ORDINARY PEOPLE CAN DO THE EXTRAORDINARY

Biblical Success Models for the African American Community

Bennie Goodwin, Ph.D.
Editor

A UMI Publication
urban ministries, inc.
Chicago, IL 60643

Publisher
Urban Ministries, Inc.
1350 West 103rd Street
Chicago, Illinois 60643
(312) 233-4499

First Edition
First Printing
ISBN: 0-940955-22-9
Catalog No. 3-2734

Scripture quotations are from the King James Version of the Bible unless otherwise stated. Printed in the United States of America.

DEDICATION

To the thousands of people who lead Bible studies in churches throughout the world.

CONTENTS

ACKNOWLEDGMENTS   6

PREFACE   *Dr. Colleen Birchett*   7

INTRODUCTION   *Dr. Bennie Goodwin*   11

I.   Micah: Brother, Where Are Your Clothes?
                             Dr. John Little   13
II.   Hosea: What's Love Got to Do With It?
                             Prof. Marvin Goodwin   21
III.   Amos: Fruit Mixed With Poetry
                             Chaplain Andrew Calhoun   33
IV.   Abraham: From the Ghetto to Greatness
                             Rabbi Sanford H. Shudnow   45
V.   Moses: Let My People Go!
                             Rabbi Sanford H. Shudnow   55
VI.   Deborah: Sister, Take Charge!
                             Chaplain Melody Goodwin   69
VII.   Samuel: The Man in the Middle
                             Mark Jeffers   81
VIII.   David: A Boy from the 'Hood
                             Chaplain Melody Goodwin   95
IX.   Solomon: Lord, Give Me Common Sense
                             Janifer Campbell   107
X.   Elijah: Strange But Powerful
                             Dr. Kenneth Hammonds   119
XI.   Josiah: It's Not Where You Come From
                             Dr. Bennie Goodwin   131
XII.   Jeremiah: Hope in Spite of Tears
                             Dr. Kenneth Hammonds   145

Footnotes   156
Bibliography   159
Biographies   IBC

ACKNOWLEDGMENTS

We wish to acknowledge the outstanding contributions of publications manager and designer, Shawan Brand; copy editor, Mary C. Lewis; and publications assistants Carolyn Cummings, Caron B. Davis and Cheryl Wilson, without whose help this book could not have come into existence. Last but not least, we wish to thank Media Graphics Corporation and Dickinson Press, Inc.

PREFACE

Dr. Colleen Birchett

The Old Testament is filled with interesting biographies. In these life stories, one can read about the ways in which God became very personal to individuals in very personal situations. From these stories, one can draw parallels and spiritual principles which can be applied in the 20th century, for every phase of the human life cycle.

Ordinary People Can Do the Extraordinary presents an overview of 12 biblical biographies. Each chapter provides an overview of a given biblical character's life, and includes questions to help the reader abstract principles from the person's life and apply them to life among African Americans today. The characters are found in a variety of political, economic and spiritual circumstances. One common thread is that these great men and women of God loved the Lord because He heard their cry.

Objectives. Upon completion of this book, the reader should be able to discuss the lives of 12 biblical characters, discuss spiritual principles which their lives teach, and explain ways in which these principles apply to life among African Americans in the 20th century. A goal of the book is to stimulate more in–depth Bible study of the lives of the characters featured in the book, and the lives of other characters of the Old and New Testaments.

Organization. With the exception of the introduction, each chapter is divided into five parts. The first part contains a "Let's Discover" section, designed to arouse interest. The second part contains a more detailed "Introduction" and a exposition of the lesson. The third part is the "Scripture Focus," with a Scripture passage related to the particular chapter. The fourth part, "Scripture Search" contains five factual questions or activities from the Scripture. The fifth part, "The African American Connection" relates the topic of the chapter to the African American experience.

Uses. The book can be used for private as well as group study. It can be used in a variety of ways in the local church: a) training of teachers and deacons; b) Sunday School electives; c) Training Hour curriculum; d) weekday Bible studies; e) Vacation Bible School curriculum for the adult class; f) family devotions.

Group Study – 90 Minute Sessions. The book is designed for a two-part group study session. Part I would allow participants to study the exposition of a Bible character's life, and to answer together the factual questions at the end of each chapter. A session leader would then divide the group into smaller groups and allow them, during Part II, to discuss the questions under the "African American Connection."

The small group discussions provide every participant the opportunity to contribute to the group's understanding and application of the material being presented. A different question from the "African American Connection" questions would be assigned to each small group. About 20 minutes should be allowed for small groups to discuss the various questions. Then they should reconvene with the larger group and report their findings.

Group Study – 60 Minute Sessions. In shorter periods, it might be necessary to use part of a given chapter as a stimulus for discussion during the group meeting itself. Then the other part of the chapter might be used as a "homework" assignment or for private devotional study.

Family Devotions. During the week preceding the study of a given chapter, all members would read a given chapter privately. However, each family member would be assigned a different question from among the "African American Connection" questions. When it is time to have devotions, each family member would provide an overview of a chapter. Then, "round robin" style, each member would read his/her assigned question and then present his/her opinion concerning "The African American Connection."

8

The Leader Guide. The Leader Guide is designed to help assist leaders of large and small group discussions related to the book, *Ordinary People Can Do the Extraordinary.* The guide contains an introductory chapter on leading group discussions. It also contains lesson plans—one for discussing each chapter.

Summary. The book can be used in a variety of ways. However, the main objective is that Christians learn important spiritual truths from the lives of great men and women of God, and apply those truths to their lives in the 20th century.

INTRODUCTION

Dr. Bennie Goodwin

Where can you find some of the richest, most famous and exciting people who ever lived? Where can you find men and women who made a positive difference in the world? Where can you find people like you and me who allowed the Lord to use their gifts, talents, knowledge and skills to enhance the lives of the poor, the sick, the down-trodden and dispossessed? Where? In the Bible, of course!

In *Ordinary People Can Do the Extraordinary,* you'll read about 12 of these people—young people and older people, good people and not-always-so-good people, city people and farmers, preachers and government administrators, poets and musicians, the courageous and cry babies.

Some of these people were Jesus' heroes—people He learned about in the synagogue. Some of them He quoted as He preached and taught, others He never mentioned, but we see parallels between what they did and what He said.

These are some of the most interesting, intriguing and challenging Black people who ever lived, and yet they are so much like us--they ate and slept, laughed and cried, were laughed at, ignored, mistreated and put down. Some were single, others were married with children who got into trouble and didn't "turn out" right. Others were children from bad home situations who "turned out" wonderfully.

They were ordinary people with ordinary problems and potential whom God used in extraordinary ways. They were just the kind of people we need to focus on to help us through these turbulent '90s, aren't they? These are the kind of folk we need to help us cope with the pressing problems of crime, teen pregnancies, gang wars, drug addiction and AIDS in our communities. These are folk that God can use to help us struggle with our personal and financial insecurities, our "besetting sins," and our home and church challenges. We believe you'll agree this book is right on time.

Each exciting chapter is divided into five major parts: "Let's Discover," "Introduction," "Scripture Focus," "Scripture Search," and "The African American Connection."

Our fervent prayer is that one of the final outcomes of this book will be ACTION that will help us to be God's agents for positive, personal and community change. Our prayer is that the Lord will use this book to help His people be the links between the power of God and the problems of people.

CHAPTER ONE

BROTHER, WHERE ARE YOUR CLOTHES?

LET'S DISCOVER . . .

Can God use an actor, a dramatist crying in the streets without clothes, to show God's people their sorrow and insecurity?
Let's discover how God uses unusual methods to remind us that God wants justice, kindness and humility.

MICAH:
Brother, Where Are Your Clothes?

Dr. John Little
Micah 1:1-4; 4:1-5; 6:6-8; 7:18-19

Micah was a prophet from Judah, who lived in the 8th century, a time when Jotham, Ahaz and Hezekiah were kings of Judah. He came from the village of Shephelah, Moresheth in the foothills of southwest Palestine (Micah 1:1). His name means "who is like God?"

The rural location of the prophet's home may explain two prominent characteristics of his message: (1) he loved poor farmers and shepherds and felt that these humble people were the backbone of the nation; (2) he observed international affairs in a manner which was natural for a dweller of a village on the route of foreign invaders.

The Word of the Lord that came to Micah was not produced by some ecstatic, out of this world experience but had a practical, "everyday" down–to–earth quality.

We do not know when Micah was born, nor when he died. But we do know that he lived and prophesied during some of the same years as Isaiah (Isaiah 1:1). We also know that the reign of Jotham (750–735 A.D.), Ahaz (735–715 A.D.) and Hezekiah (715–687 A.D.) were times of prosperity and that the Jews were not serving God as they had promised.

Under these circumstances Micah preached in Jerusalem so dynamically that he, like Isaiah, influenced Hezekiah and led him to inaugurate a reform which later inspired the reform of Josiah (Jeremiah 26:16–19). Micah's concern was to let his fel-

14

low Jews know that unless they made some changes they would suffer the same defeat as the Northern Kingdom of Israel (Micah 1:5–6; 2 Kings 17:6). The extent of the prophet's concern and conviction dictated the intensity of his activity.

Micah's Time

Micah refused to be lulled into complacency. The conditions of his time were most abject. The rulers of the house of Israel hated what was good and loved what was evil. Many of Jerusalem's civil officials had become criminals. The judges' hands itched for bribes, the priests said what people wanted to hear in order to enrich themselves, and the prophets had forsaken their sacred calling as spokespersons for the Lord. Corruption of the most base nature was the order of the day.

Of the business owners, Micah said, "they work evil upon their beds, they turn the chamber of their sleep into a place for plotting and abuse. When day comes the plot materializes at the expense of the poor" (Micah 2:1). Their sense of conscience and shame was lost in the quest of unlawful gain.

At the administrative level of the government, people's eyes were closed by greed. Bribery was rampant, and the trust needed for the administration of fairness and justice was perverted. Might not right regulated the administration's conduct. They disregarded the law and no deed was too atrocious for the success of their selfish ventures. The downward sequence was first they sinned in thought, then in desire and afterward in action. They oppressed men and seized their houses, ruining whole families (2:2).

By this commitment to please the rich and corrupt, the religious leaders had forsaken their task of speaking for God. They misrepresented God and His Word and pretended to be inspired. The false prophets promoted self–indulgence by promising abundant harvests and lush vintages, in spite of the people's sins. False teachers pandered to baseness, sanctioned sinful customs and completely failed to prick the people's conscience. Micah reproved the rulers of the nation, civil and religious,

15

summed up their sins and declared that none would escape the judgment of God.

Micah's Method

Micah's picturesque use of words usually expressed in the language of his rural background. He talked about mountains, valleys and waterfalls, wax and fire, heaps in the fields, and planting of vineyards (1:3–6). To get his message across he used descriptive words like plowshares and pruning hooks, vines and fig trees, and sheaves on a threshing floor (4:3–4, 12). He pictured shepherds and sheep, lions and beasts of the forest, dew and showers on the grass, (5:5–14), as well as calves and rams (6:6), summer fruit, grapes, briers, thorns, serpents and worms (7:1–17). Micah said things in such a way that you could visualize it in your "mind's eye."

But he went further—he dramatized his message. Because of the intensity of his convictions, Micah was willing to imitate some of the animal sounds he talked about. He said, "I will wail and howl, I will go stripped and naked: I will make a wailing like the dragons, and mourning as the owls" (1:8).

The brother was serious. Could anybody miss Micah's message? Even the blind could hear it and the deaf could see it. Micah loved his people and wanted to make sure everybody was alerted to the critical situation and impending doom. "For the nation's wound is incurable...therefore thus saith the Lord, behold, against this family do I devise evil...for this time is evil" (1:9; 2:3).

Micah's Message

A. God Is Present. Against this backdrop of corruption, Micah declared that God is not an idle observer and will not delay punishment indefinitely. He confirmed that God is moved to act when the leaders poison the stream of life and turn it into a deadly fountain. God is not an idle observer in human history but a meaningful participant. When righteousness is on the throne,

God assures us that all the powers of heaven and earth are mobilized to move in our best interest. But when we become contrary to the will of God, we invite doom and disaster. God allows captivity to exert correction. He permits disaster to prompt discipline. He uses the rod that it may bring forth righteousness. God is involved in human history.

B. God Is Power. Micah preached that God is present, knows all and is involved in events; furthermore, God has the power to bring about change. The prophet declared that God's power enabled and inspired him to deliver his message. "I am filled with power," he proclaimed (3:8). It was a force instilled by God.

Micah could have been dealing in mischief, along with the false prophets and teachers, but his relationship with God and his love for his nation would not allow him. God was in charge of his life, and God always raises up a nation or a person who will obey. Micah had "soul power" and expressed it in his words and deeds. He was not noted as a powerful intellect, nor as a charismatic personality, but he was filled with power–the power of God.

C. God Is Hope. Micah's message is not all "gloom and doom." Through him, God spoke words of hope. The nation of Israel will one day be a gathering place of nations and there will be a time of universal peace (4:1–3). The birth of Jesus, the Messiah will take place in Bethlehem (5:2) and the Jewish people, then so prone to idol worship, will one day turn from practices of witchcraft, and idolatry will cease (5:12–14). Micah declared that out of the nation's dark present God will bring a bright future.

D. God Is Love. Yes, we have sinned, the Book of Micah reminds us, but God is not impressed with our works or sacrifices. His requirements are not complex. He wants us to do what is right, to show mercy to those who deserve justice and to maintain an attitude toward Him that is consistent with who He is and what He has done for us (6:6–8).

Yes, we are sinners, but God loves us. He does not hold grudges against us, but looks at us through eyes of compassion, shows us mercy and forgives our sins. Who is a God like Him? (7:18–19)

17

SCRIPTURE FOCUS

MICAH 1:1 The Word of the Lord that came to Micah the Morasthite in the days of Jotham, Ahaz, and Hezekiah, kings of Judah, which he saw concerning Samaria and Jerusalem.

2 Hear, all ye people; hearken, O earth, and all that therein is: and let the Lord God be witness against you, the Lord from his holy temple.

3 For, behold, the Lord cometh forth out of his place, and will come down, and tread upon the high places of the earth.

4 And the mountains shall be molten under him, and the valleys shall be cleft, as wax before the fire, and as the waters that are poured down a steep place.

MICAH 4:1 But in the last days it shall come to pass, that the mountain of the house of the Lord shall be established in the top of the mountains, and it shall be exalted above the hills; and people shall flow unto it.

2 And many nations shall come, and say, Come, and let us go up to the mountain of the Lord, and to the house of the God of Jacob; and he will teach us of his ways, and we will walk in his paths: for the law shall go forth of Zion, and the word of the Lord from Jerusalem.

3 And he shall judge among many people, and rebuke strong nations afar off; and they shall beat their swords into plowshares, and their spears into pruning hooks: nation shall not lift up a sword against nation, neither shall they learn war any more.

4 But they shall sit every man under his vine and under his fig tree; and none shall make them afraid: for the mouth of the Lord of hosts hath spoken it.

5 For all people will walk every one in the name

of his god, and we will walk in the name of the Lord our God for ever and ever.

MICAH 6:6 Wherewith shall I come before the Lord, and bow myself before the high God? shall I come before him with burnt offerings, with calves of a year old?

7 Will the Lord be pleased with thousands of rams, or with ten thousands of rivers of oil? shall I give my firstborn for my transgression, the fruit of my body for the sin of my soul?

8 He hath shown thee, O man, what is good; and what doth the Lord require of thee, but to do justly, and to love mercy, and to walk humbly with thy God?

MICAH 7:18 Who is a God like unto thee, that pardoneth iniquity, and passeth by the transgression of the remnant of his heritage? he retaineth not his anger for ever, because he delighteth in mercy.

19 He will turn again, he will have compassion upon us; he will subdue our iniquities; and thou wilt cast all their sins into the depths of the sea.

SCRIPTURE SEARCH

1. Micah was…
   a) a musician b) a dramatist c) an engineer

2. Micah was…
   a) a priest b) a prophet c) a king

3. Micah was from…
   a) Judah b) Israel c) Ninevah

4. Micah preached to a society that was…
   a) God-fearing b) compassionate c) corrupt

5. Micah preached that in spite of the condition of his society, God is…
a) present b) powerful c) hope d) love e) all four

The African American Connection

1. Communicate Clearly
Barbara Jordan, Jesse Jackson and Dr. Martin Luther King, Jr. are recognized for their effective communication skills. a) In what ways do they remind us of the Prophet Micah? b) Is there a relationship between effective communication skills and effective leadership? If so, what is the relationship? c) Why should we encourage our young people to develop skill in speaking standard English in addition to Black English? d) Give three reasons why it is important to communicate effectively when we witness to our faith in Christ.

2. Lead Unofficially
Dr. Martin Luther King, Jr. was approached but refused to run for president of the United States. He felt he could do more good for his people by not holding political office. a) Did he make the right decision? b) Could Micah have made a greater impact as a priest, an "official prophet" or a member of the king's court? c) What are some advantages: 1) of working within the system, as did Andrew Young and Josiah? 2) of working outside the system, as did Dr. King and Micah?

3. Take Risks
Socrates, Gandhi, Medgar Evers and Malcolm X–each of these men spoke their convictions and was assassinated. With our high infant mortality, teenage homicide and prison population rates: a) Can we afford to encourage our people to risk assassination for speaking out against social oppression and economic injustice? b) Can we afford to encourage silence?

CHAPTER TWO

WHAT'S LOVE GOT TO DO WITH IT?

LET'S DISCOVER . . .

Can God use a prostitute to help a prophet understand His love and kindness, His patience and forgiveness? Let's discover how God uses "bad" people to teach lessons to "good" people, to a society gone wrong, to a nation He loves.

HOSEA:
What's Love Got to Do With It?

Professor Marvin Goodwin
Hosea 1:1-4, 6-9; 3:1-5; 6:1-3

The name "Hosea" means salvation. The Book of Hosea is the first in a series of books by a group called the 12 minor prophets. This does not mean that the "minor" prophets are less important than the "major" prophets. It means that their books are shorter in length.

Hosea is believed to be a contemporary of the Prophet Amos. His work is divided into two parts. The first part, chapters one through three, comprises both the biographical and autobiographical dimensions of the little book. It is biographical because Hosea speaks for God. It is autobiographical because he relates his own experiences. The second part, chapters four through fourteen, comprises the spiritual dimension of the book.

The Book of Hosea contains one of world literature's most profound and tragic love stories. It proves God's ability to use the circumstances of a life to provide a greater lesson of His enduring love.

Hosea the Man
Beyond what is given in chapters one through three, little is known about Hosea. We are told that his father was Beeri (Hosea 1:1) but where he lived, what he did before being called to prophesy or when he was called are all features left to our imagination.

However, from his writings we gain some insights into Hosea's personality. He was well versed on Israel's political and religious situation. It is also obvious from his writings that he was a man of ability and culture. He had a grasp of the literature of his day, was thoroughly steeped in Israel's historical tradition and understood that the prophet was God's primary instrument in dealing with His people, Israel.

James Mays points out: "Hosea thought of the prophet as the mouth of God (1:1-2). Accordingly his sayings are predominantly spoken in the first person of divine speech. On occasion he speaks in his own right in prophetic sayings, but one frequently has the feeling that Hosea is so personally identified with his God that shifts to third–person references to Yahweh do not fundamentally interrupt the actuality of his function as God's spokesman."[1] For Hosea, the prophet was one who fought for God against the worship of the idol god Baal, the king and his alliances with foreign military powers. His message was directed primarily at the Northern Kingdom of Israel. He uses the name "Ephraim" 36 times to refer to the Northern Kingdom.

Hosea's Wife

The Prophet Hosea totally identifies with God. This is especially apparent in chapters 1 and 3. In chapter one he is given a command to marry a "wife of whoredom" or "harlotry" (1:2). Bible scholars have interpreted "wife of harlotry" in three ways: 1) to show God's intimate relationship with Israel; 2) Gomer had fallen into an immoral life *after* Hosea married her; and 3) to indicate that Hosea knew Gomer was a prostitute *when* he married her. A simple direct reading of the text suggests that the third view is probably the correct one.

Religion in Israel had been debased by the worship of Baal. In Baalism, both men and women engaged in sexual relationships as part of their worship. A "wife of whoredom" probably designated an ordinary Hebrew woman of that time who had offered her body in the worship of Baal, not one who made a living as a common prostitute. For a man such as Hosea, whose sensitivity emerges from every page of his book, the command to marry a woman of whoredom was extraordinary and a most unusual form of prophetic vocation.

23

Hosea's Call

The reason for God's call to His prophet is quickly given: "for the land has committed great harlotry" (1:2). From the very beginning the connection between Hosea's personal experience and that of God is seen. The major themes of the Book of Hosea are illustrated in his personal experiences.

The prophet is commanded, "Go again, love a woman who is loved by a lover..." (3:1). This verse has caused much controversy among scholars regarding the identity of the woman Hosea is commanded to love. Is she Gomer or is this another woman? Perhaps they are one and the same. The Lord has renewed His call to Hosea to love his wife despite the fact that she has returned to her former immoral life–style.

Hosea's Times

The career of the Prophet Hosea began during the reign of King Jeroboam II, a time of great prosperity and peace. It ended with Israel moving swiftly toward slavery in Babylon.

The events and conditions of the period, 750–722 A.D. are reflected vividly in Hosea's writings. At the time Hosea names his son Jezreel, Jeroboam II, the great–grandson of Jehu, was on the throne. During his reign Hosea's marriage to Gomer and the birth of their three children took place. Much of what is said in Hosea 1—3 mirrors the early years of Jeroboam's rule. These were years of political stability, economic prosperity, and vigorous religious observance (1:2–9; 2:2–15). But this did not last and Hosea foretold the coming doom.

Shortly after ascending the throne, Zechariah, son of Jeroboam II, was murdered by the usurper Shallum, who in turn was assassinated by Menahem. Thereafter, Israel was governed by the politics of conspiracy and assassinations. Only one of the kings who succeeded Jeroboam II, Menahem, died a natural death.

In their desperation to hold on to power, Israel's kings sought foreign help, paying tribute alternately to Assyria and then

Egypt. They did not seek the God of their fathers for He was no longer meaningful to them. Israel's leaders and people were morally diseased and spiritually bankrupt.

Their political policy was no remedy for their moral decline which had affected the priesthood (8:9; 10:6). Those who should have been pointing the nation toward God as the source of healing and deliverance were themselves in need of healing. They had caused Israel to backslide. Because it increased their revenues, priests had turned into bandits and rejoiced in the sins of the people. Things had gotten so bad that the prophet exclaims in great anxiety, "There is no truth, nor goodness, nor knowledge of God in the land. By swearing and lying, killing and stealing and committing adultery, they break all restraint, with bloodshed upon bloodshed" (4:1, 2).

Hosea's Message (Chapters 4—14)

George I. Robinson has characterized Hosea's message as "one long impassioned monologue, broken by sobs."[2]

A. Israel's Condition. Hosea tells of God being deeply in love with His people who are constantly breaking His heart. Therefore, Hosea's indictments against Israel were that her sin was worse than adultery: She had played the harlot and become a prostitute for hire to Baal, the god of Canaan (2:12–13). He asserted that Israel was without knowledge and this accounted for her ignorance of God and His law (4:6; 5:4; 8:12).

While they paid honor to God with their lips, in reality they honored and served Baal. It was for their lack of honor for the true God that Hosea heaps his severest criticisms and rebukes on Israel. Reduced to its simplest terms, the indictments were: Israel had broken her covenant with Jehovah and rebelled against His instructions. Israel's entire corporate life in religion and politics was a rejection of Jehovah, and a complete betrayal of the identity which He had created for them.

That they were living in sin was nothing new. From the time of their first entry into the land of Canaan they sinned time and time again. They were continually adding sin upon sin, until their evil deeds became a way of life—the sum of their character (7:1; 4:12). Mays elaborates: "they were prisoners of their sin, trapped by the identity that they had created (5:4)."[3]

Israel's faithlessness had reached such a state that they were unrecognizable as the people of God. To illustrate this fact God instructs Hosea to name his third child *Loammi,* "Not–My–People" (1:9). They had become unidentifiable from the Canaanites because they looked and acted as though they had no knowledge of God. Their lives were devoid of God's principles and righteousness. They were God's people in name only and brought shame upon the name of God. These were the people among whom God sent Hosea to prophesy.

B. Israel's Judgment. Hosea's rebukes were focused on Israel's failures, which centered in two areas: their cults or religious life and their political life. Israel was involved in the fertility cults of Canaan. In its simplest form, those who worshiped Baal gave him credit for being the source of life. They believed that because of Baal's blessings plants, animals and people experienced life and growth. This directly contradicted the Israelites' faith in Jehovah, their God, so Hosea looked upon Baal as in a great struggle for the soul of a nation which was supposed to be committed to Jehovah. Hosea declared that there were to be two kinds of specific and fundamental judgments for the sins of Israel: judgment in relation to the fertility cult and in relation to the king's corrupt politics.

First, the fruitfulness of the land and the people's fertility, which Israel attributed to Baal, would cease (2:9–13; 4:3, 10; 8:7; 9:2, 11–14, 16). Abundant blessings would be replaced by the curse of famine, hunger and infertility.

Secondly, Israel would suffer devastating military defeat and finally political collapse (7:16; 8:3, 13; 10:6–10, 14). All of her military strategies would fail and her alliances would prove futile. All these judgments were the consequence of her unfaithful behavior. The sins of the past had caught up with her, and the sins of the present doomed her future. She had betrayed the God of her fathers and was reaping the chastisement of her betrayal (13:7; 5:14, 12).

C. God's Promise of Renewal (14:1–8). Hosea preached that although Israel was to be chastised by Jehovah, he still loved her and desired her restoration. Hosea ends his prophecy by making a plea for Israel's repentance and a promise of healing and love. Included in his call for repentance is Hosea's penitential prayer. Although he is not involved in Israel's sins he identifies with the sins of the nation (vv. 4–8). In response to Hosea's prayer, God says that if Israel would repent, turn away from Baal and return to Him, He would forgive their sins and turn away the impending disasters.

Where there would be disease, there would be healing; where His righteous indignation would be poured out upon His wayward children, there would be instead an outpouring of divine love; and instead of drought and infertility there would be an abundance of fruit. If Israel would return and dwell beneath the shadow of her God, she would come to know that it is God who takes care of her. She would then know that her fruitfulness was from the God of her fathers, and not from Baal. If she repented of her sins, she would at last learn the true knowledge of God.

SCRIPTURE FOCUS

HOSEA 1:1 The word of the Lord that came unto Hosea, the son of Beeri, in the days of Uzziah, Jotham, Ahaz, and Hezekiah, kings of Judah, and in the days of Jeroboam the son of Joash, king of Israel.

2 The beginning of the word of the Lord by Hosea. And the Lord said to Hosea, Go, take unto thee a wife of whoredoms and children of whoredoms: for the land hath committed great whoredom, departing from the Lord.

3 So he went and took Gomer the daughter of Diblaim; which conceived, and bare him a son.

4 And the Lord said unto him, Call his name Jezreel; for yet a little while, and I will avenge the blood of Jezreel upon the house of Jehu, and will cause to cease the kingdom of the house of Israel.

6 And she conceived again, and bare a daughter. And God said unto him, Call her name Lo-ruhamah: for I will no more have mercy upon the house of Israel; but I will utterly take them away.

7 But I will have mercy upon the house of Judah, and will save them by the Lord their God, and will not save them by bow, nor by sword, nor by battle, by horses, nor by horsemen.

8 Now when she had weaned Lo-ruhamah, she conceived, and bare a son.

9 Then said God, Call his name Lo-ammi: for ye are not my people, and I will not be your God.

HOSEA 3:1 Then said the Lord unto me, Go yet, love a woman beloved of her friend, yet an adulteress, according to the love of the Lord toward the children of Israel, who look to other gods, and love flagons of wine.

2 So I bought her to me for fifteen pieces of silver, and for an homer of barley, and an half homer of barley:

3 And I said unto her, Thou shalt abide for me many days; thou shalt not play the harlot, and thou shalt not be for another man: so will I also be for thee.

4 For the children of Israel shall abide many days without a king, and without a prince, and without a sacrifice, and without an image, and without an ephod, and without teraphim:

5 Afterward shall the children of Israel return, and seek the Lord their God, and David their king; and shall fear the Lord and his goodness in the latter days.

HOSEA 6:1 Come, and let us return unto the Lord: for he hath torn, and he will heal us; he hath smitten, and he will bind us up.

2 After two days will he revive us: in the third day he will raise us up, and we shall live in his sight.

3 Then shall we know, if we follow on to know the Lord; he going forth is prepared as the morning; and he shall come unto us as the rain, as the latter and former rain unto the earth.

SCRIPTURE SEARCH

Match the columns.

1. Hosea's wife
2. Hosea's name
3. Hosea's personality
4. Hosea's son
5. Israel's future

A. Jezreel
B. Defeat and restoration
C. Salvation
D. Ability, culture, sensitivity
E. Gomer, the prostitute

The African American Connection

1. The Family

The break up of the family is one of the most critical problems facing African Americans today. The African American family is under extreme pressure from forces within and without. Within the Black community is a high divorce and separation rate. As of 1991, 57% of Black families are headed by single parents,[4] and a large proportion of Black families are headed by females. The dysfunctional family, the product of the new morality, has produced many sons without nurturing fathers to provide responsible role models.

The family is one of the major concerns addressed by Hosea. The character of his leadership is seen in his sense of family responsibility. He made every effort to keep his family together. His love and sense of compassion, as well as his strength of character are clearly seen in his attempt to provide stability for his family. He does not hide from unpleasant family circumstances but instead accepts his responsibility as head of his family.

2. The Church

Historically the church has been the center of the African American community. Faith in its leadership has been strong. Usually church leaders were perceived as exemplifying high moral principles and were held in high esteem. They were sought out for their understanding, concern and compassion. Has this perception changed? Because of the failure of many of its leaders, many youth within the Black community are rejecting their heritage in the church. They no longer seek the comfort and leadership which the church provided for so long. What many persons, within the church, fail to take into account is that nations always experience a rapid decline when its religious leaders are filled with avarice and corruption; "like people, like priest" (Hosea 4:9). The church, the family and the nation are tied together. The failure of any one of the three affects the others. Where the family and the church are strong, the nation is strong.

3. What Do You Think?

A. Is it still true that our two strongest institutions are the family and the church?

B. What are three or four concrete ways that the family can strengthen the church and the church can strengthen the family?

C. What is the evidence that the African American church is the most important institution in the Black community?

D. Today, what role does the Black family play in the lives of African Americans?

E. How can churches build communities?

4. Books Recommended

How to Equip the African American Family, by Drs. George and Yvonne Abatso (Chicago: Urban Ministries, 1991); and *The Church in the Life of the Black Family,* by Wallace Charles Smith (Valley Forge: Judson Press, 1985).

CHAPTER THREE

FRUIT MIXED WITH POETRY

L*ET'S* D*ISCOVER* . . .

*Can God use a farmer to help city folk
get a new self-image, to help justice run
down freely like water, to help doing right
flow like a mighty stream?
Let's discover how God uses rural
people to help urban folk see ourselves as
God sees us, and to bring our walk in line
with our talk.*

AMOS:
Fruit Mixed with Poetry

Chaplain Andrew Calhoun
Amos 1:1-2; 3:1-8; 7:14-15; 9:13-15

"A voice for the times" best describes the ministry of Amos to God's chosen people. He stands as God's messenger in a difficult hour in the history of Israel and Judah. He had a call, a conviction and a powerful message. God called Amos to deliver words of doom and destruction, restoration and hope. As a common man, he was in touch with the political, social and religious conditions of his times.

The name Amos means "burden bearer." It comes from the Hebrew root word *amas,* which means "to carry." The Book of Amos does not provide any personal or family background information about him. The time of his birth and death are unknown. In one sense the prophet is a mystery, but he stands as the most colorful personality among the minor prophets.

Amos's Calling and Commission
Amos came from Tekoa, a small village about ten miles south of Jerusalem. Tekoa, located in the heart of Judah, was a wild, desolate desert area.

The setting of central Judah provides a very unusual place for the calling of a prophet. Who would expect God to call a person from this area to be His voice? The main occupations for Tekoa were sheep herding and fruit growing. Amos describes himself as a shepherd and picker of sycamore figs (Amos 7:14).

Amos had a problem being a prophet. When Amos traveled to the shrine city of Bethel, he was confronted by Amaziah the high priest who was disturbed by his message. Amaziah told Amos, "O seer, go flee away to the land of Judah and eat bread there, and prophesy there; but never again prophesy at Bethel for it is the king's sanctuary, and it is the temple of the kingdom" (7:12–13). Amos quickly informed the high priest of his credentials: "I was not a prophet nor a son of a prophet, but a herdsman and dresser of sycamore trees. And the Lord took me from following the flock, and the Lord said to me, Go, prophesy to my people Israel" (7:14–15).

We can assume from the conversation that Amos did not attend the "School of the Prophets" or receive training from other prophets. He seems to have been called by God and prepared for his unique mission by experience and special revelations.

Sizemore states: "We do not have a biography or personality analysis of Amos. However, we do have stirring and demanding words which reflect a courageous and creative mind seized and empowered by the hand of God."[1] Kyle M. Yates states: "In any emergency God can raise up an effective prophet to do His will."[2] In any case Amos is God's man for the hour. In Amos we see a profile of a common man called by God to carry a special message.

Amos's Context for Ministry

The Book of Amos comes from the middle of the 8th century B.C. The two Hebrew kingdoms had stood divided for 175 years. For both kingdoms it was a time of security and peace. However, it also marked the beginning of Israel's decline.

Amos carried on his ministry from about 760–750 B.C. This placed his ministry during the time when King Jeroboam II reigned over Israel, Uzziah reigned as king of Judah, and Ashurban III was king of Assyria.

Politically, Israel enjoyed a time of great peace and security. Their stability came as a result of many neighbors having internal problems. Even Israel's greatest threats, Assyria and Syria, were at war with each other.

Under the leadership of King Jeroboam II, Israel became strong and rich again. Israel regained all of its territory and splendor. The last time the nation enjoyed such prosperity was in the days of King Solomon. With peace and prosperity in the land, the people believed that God was smiling on them.

Socially, the rich became wealthier at the expense of the poor. The rich took advantage of the nation's stability and improved their businesses through increased trade and commerce. Their businesses were good and labor was cheap.

The wealthy lived a life of luxury. They had vacation homes along the sea and winter homes in the mountains. These homes were built of the best materials money could buy. They slept in the finest beds and had the best to eat. In other words the rich got richer, while the poor got poorer.

The impoverished of the nation experienced many problems. They were being oppressed and exploited. The poor could not get justice in the marketplaces or the courts. They were being sold for a pair of shoes (2:6). Scales were rigged in the markets and judges were on the take. This was a nation divided between the "haves and have nots."

The increased wealth, peace, territorial expansion, and prosperity did not bring spiritual renewal. The people were unfaithful to God. Yates states: "The people practiced worship that insulted God."[3] They gave their allegiance to the golden calves at shrines in the cities of Bethel and Dan.

Many people practiced a false religion propagated by Amaziah, the high priest, who also supported political and social corruption. These were dismal days for the common people.

Amos was alert to his social environment and had a clear insight into the conditions of his time. Undoubtedly his early environment and occupation helped prepare him for his mission. These and other factors contributed to his character development and aided in cultivating the qualities necessary for effective leadership.

Amos's Message to Israel

Amos's message is a cry for universal justice. Amos makes this issue clear in summarizing the sins of Israel, its neighbors and enemies (1—2:5). From Amos's standpoint, Israel and all her neighbors were guilty of moral and social misconduct.

The prophet provides a list of those nations and their sins against humanity. These sins include: inhuman treatment, hatred, unbrotherly conduct, cruelty in war, oppression of people and slavery. He pronounces God's punishment for each nation. The people of Israel rejoice as Amos tells of their neighbors' punishment. However, their rejoicing quickly turns into anger, as Amos begins to tell of their sins.

Amos proclaims to the people of Israel that they are like their neighbors (2:6–8). They stand guilty of many sins, including the inhuman treatment of the poor. He declares further that their sins are worse than those of their neighbors. In fact, their greatest sin was being unfaithful to God.

Amos tells the people of Israel that they are guilty of three crimes: 1) they did not heed previous warnings, 2) they have practiced empty worship and 3) they have committed acts of gross injustice (4:4–14; 5:21–27). He boldly declares that the dark day of the Lord is now upon them. Israel must now choose the right path or face the wrath of God.

Amos's message falls naturally into two parts. In the first part he reminds his hearers of their sins and God's chastisement. God said that He will "shake the house of Israel and purge out the sinners among His people" (9:9). In the second part of the message, God promises to restore the fortunes of His people (9:13–15). The second portion of Amos's message is a proclamation of restoration and hope.

Amos's Leadership Qualities

The leadership style of Amos is unique. It is a very strong style of leadership for a very difficult religious and social era. Amos was both bold and confrontational.

The Prophet Amos reflects several leadership qualities. These include: courage, dependability, endurance, enthusiasm, integrity, knowledge and loyalty.

A. Amos Was Courageous. His courage is seen in his traveling from Tekoa, Judah to Israel. He had the courage to take God's message directly to Israel. Amos confronted Israel's leadership with God's message, withstanding even the challenge of Amaziah, the high priest. He was a man of courage.

B. Amos Was Dependable. God needed someone He could trust. Amos's dependability is seen in his actions. He left his occupation and traveled to Israel to deliver the message that God gave him and did not leave Israel until he had finished his mission. Effective leadership and dependability are closely connected.

C. Amos Had the Ability to Endure. He possessed mental and physical stamina. He endured the pressure of speaking an unpopular message to the people of Israel and the threats from the high priest. Some believe that this quality was probably developed during his rural upbringing and his time spent as a shepherd and fruit grower. An effective leader is able to endure opposition. Obstacles are almost a constant part of a leader's life.

D. Amos Was Enthusiastic. He had the zeal to carry out God's directives. He spoke to Israel with the power of God. God had called him to carry a special message to Israel and he did so without complaining or hesitating. Willingness to give the best effort in fulfilling a mission is one of the marks of an effective leader.

E. Amos Was a Man of Integrity. He was a moral and honest man. He spoke the will of God to the nation of Israel from his heart. The prophet did not care about the feelings of the rich or powerful in Israel. He told them the truth and did not hold back.

F. Amos Exhibited Knowledge. Amos knew what was going on in Israel and in the surrounding nations. He picked specific examples of inhuman treatment and sin. He was very much aware of the problems of the poor and oppressed. Amos might have become aware of the vast political and social problems of each nation through his travels to various marketplaces. Effective leaders are aware of people's problems and potentials—as individuals and as a society. An effective leader must be "in the know."

G. Amos Was Loyal. His loyalty was reflected in his commitment to speak on God's behalf. Amos did not travel to Israel proclaiming God's word because of personal ambition. He went to fulfill his calling. The commission to be a Christian leader requires loyalty to God, God's people and his God–given task.

SCRIPTURE FOCUS

AMOS 1:1 The Words of Amos, who was among the herdmen of Tekoa, which he saw concerning Israel in the days of Uzziah king of Judah, and in the days of Jeroboam the son of Joash king of Israel, two years before the earthquake.

2 And he said, the Lord will roar from Zion, and utter his voice from Jerusalem; and the habitations of the shepherds shall mourn, and the top of Carmel shall wither.

AMOS 3:1 Hear this word that the Lord hath spoken against you, O children of Israel, against the whole family which I brought up from the land of Egypt, saying,

2 You only have I known of all the families of the earth: therefore I will punish you for all your iniquities.

3 Can two walk together, except they be agreed?

4 Will a lion roar in the forest, when he hath no prey? will a young lion cry out of his den, if he have taken nothing?

5 Can a bird fall in a snare upon the earth, where no gin is for him? shall one take up a snare from the earth, and have taken nothing at all?

6 Shall a trumpet be blown in the city, and the people not be afraid? shall there be evil in a city, and the Lord hath not done it?

7 Surely the Lord God will do nothing, but he revealeth his secret unto his servants the prophets.

8 The lion hath roared, who will not fear? the Lord God hath spoken, who can but prophesy?

AMOS 7:14 Then answered Amos, and said to Amaziah, I was no prophet, neither was I a prophet's son; but I was an herdman, and a gatherer of sycamore fruit:

15 And the Lord took me as I followed the flock, and the Lord said unto me, Go, prophesy unto my people Israel.

AMOS 9:13 Behold, the days come, saith the Lord, that the plowman shall overtake the reaper, and the treader of grapes him that soweth seed; and the mountains shall drop sweet wine, and all the hills shall melt.

14 And I will bring again the captivity of my people of Israel, and they shall build the waste cities, and inhabit them; and they shall plant vineyards, and drink the wine thereof; they shall also make gardens, and eat the fruit of them.

15 And I will plant them upon their land, and they shall no more be pulled up out of their land which I have given them, saith the Lord thy God.

SCRIPTURE SEARCH

Fill in the blanks.

1. Amos was a _____ by occupation.
2. Amos accused his society of empty _____ and gross injustices.
3. Amos was a leader who was courageous, _____ and dependable.
4. Amos preached a message of doom and destruction, restoration and _____.
5. Amos wanted justice to run down like _____ and righteousness as a mighty _____.

The African American Connection

The problems of the African American community exist in four basic areas: economics, education, politics and anti–social behavior. Some of the problems within one area develop as a direct result of problems existing in another area. Solutions to many of these problems are complex and difficult. Some problems can be addressed through fair government policies; however, other problems will require empowering communities to help themselves.

1. Economics

Economics is one of the major problem areas we face. The economic factor is an underlying cause for other problems. The African American community is a $130 billion a year community. However, only a small percent of this revenue is recycled through the community.

What are two or three ways that we can give money a longer circulation life in our communities? Is an increase in Black businesses the answer? Is a "buy Black" campaign a possible solution? Will forming community co–ops help? If we boycott certain banks, will this help stop some of the "red lining" that is often practiced against our communities?

2. Education

African Americans are seeing a weakening of the public education system. This is due in part to the emergence of rich and poor school districts. This kind of development reflects another kind of segregation. Rich school districts tend to be in the suburbs and poor districts are usually in the inner city where many of our people live. The condition of housing has often deteriorated in these areas and they are sometimes controlled by slum landlords. With limited funding, increasing expenses and high enrollment, poor school districts do not keep up with the rising cost of educating students.

To add to this problem, a high number of African American youth continue to drop out of school. This adds to the problems of unemployment, which aggravates other social problems such as crime, drug addiction and homelessness.

Are these possible answers to our educational dilemma? More Black teachers and administrators in charge of our schools? More involvement of our parents in the Parent Teachers Association (PTA)? More security personnel in our schools to insure the safety of our students and school staff?

3. Politics

The third major area of concern is politics. Politically the African American community is suffering.

What effect do such things as lack of voting, redistricting and lack of qualified candidates who are willing to run for office have on our political situation?

4. Anti–Social Behavior

Finally, many African American communities are facing an array of problems with anti–social behavior such as crime and drug abuse. There is a continued rise of Black on Black crime. The illegal drug business continues to cause a rise in crime and violence. In this dangerous illegal business many young

Black boys and men are being killed daily and an alarming number of young Blacks are being incarcerated. What can African American Christians do about this?

In what ways could our recommitment to God and the church, our decision to begin speaking out, and our taking initiative to make positive changes make a difference in the amount of drugs sold and used in our neighborhood?

Can the Lord make a difference through our churches? Or is the church doomed to stand by and let the devil completely take over our communities?

CHAPTER FOUR

FROM THE GHETTO TO GREATNESS

Let's Discover . . .

Can God use an ordinary pagan, an idol worshiper, as father of a new people, to enjoy a new relationship, receive a new promise, envision a new homeland?
Let's discover how God can use a person to change people from having a spiritually poor home and neighborhood to accomplishing an extraordinary task.

ABRAHAM:
From the Ghetto to Greatness

Rabbi Sanford H. Shudnow
Genesis 12:1-8; Hebrews 11:8-12

African American Christians have always turned to the Old Testament for direction and solace in times of turmoil. This is quite evident in some Negro spirituals. Often the emphasis was on identification with the Israelites in their enslavement in Egypt and their liberation from bondage through the Exodus. But the Exodus experience is only one of many points of identification. Abraham's experience of uprootedness and calling by the Almighty to serve Him as leader of a nation and of many nations in a new land is also quite relevant.

What's in a Name?
Today, names are chosen often because they remind us of our relatives or close friends, or because the name sounds beautiful and we like it. In the biblical practice of naming, each name and name change marked a trait or expectation of the specific individual.

When we first meet Abraham his name is Abram or *Avram* in the original Hebrew. Avram is composed of two syllables, each a word—*Av* (father) and *ram* (lofty, high). Since Abraham or Abram is to be the father of the chosen people of God, his name is a prophecy of the future.

Later, Abram's name will be changed to Abraham or *Avraham,* demonstrating an increased status and responsibility. He becomes father of many nations through his son Ishmael.

Abraham's Birth and Background

Abram was born in Ur, a city of high culture and commerce on the Persian Gulf. Scripture speaks of Terah, Abram's father and the family leaving Ur and migrating to Haran (Genesis 11:31). The estimated date of their journey was 1800 B.C.E.

Abram is known in the Bible as Ha–Ivri, the Hebrew (14:13). Ivri derives from *Ever,* which means "crossing" and is employed to show that Abram and his people crossed over from the other side of the Rivers Tigris and Euphrates into Canaan, later to be called Israel, the new name given by Abraham's grandson Jacob.

Our knowledge of Abraham and his active life spans 100 years from his call from God, "Leave your country, your people and your father's household and go to the land I will show you" (12:1). He died at the age of 175, buried by his sons Isaac and Ishmael.

When Abram set out upon his journey, "He took his wife Sarai, his nephew Lot, all the possessions they had accumulated and the people they had acquired in Haran" (12:5). Rabbinic tradition understands the phrase, "the people they had acquired…" to mean converts to the new faith.[1]

Abraham as Husband

Abraham set a precedent for the modern concept of marriage and the relationship between husband and wife. The status of the woman as mere property in the ancient Near East has been well documented. While the Bible is often criticized regarding the status of women, in some cases the Bible raises that status to a very high degree.

Abraham treats Sarah as a blood relative and considers her as close as a sister. He presents her as such on at least two occasions to Pharaoh and Abimelekh. We see Abraham and Sarah conversing as equals. At the point when God calls Abraham to sacrifice his son on Mount Moriah, formally known as the "Binding of Isaac," Abraham is considerate of Sarah's feelings, concealing from her this last supreme trial that God has placed before him, that may bring the death of Sarah's only son (22:1f).

47

Abraham, Example of Hospitality

Abraham's treatment of the three visitors or angels who came to his tent (Genesis 18), illustrates the value he places on hospitality. He had just undergone painful circumcision in his old age. He was sitting at the entrance of his tent near a tree, seeking some relief from the heat of the day. At this very moment three visitors approach him. Instead of attempting to avoid the strangers, Abraham hurries to receive them, "bowing low to the ground" in respect (18:2). He does everything in his power to persuade his guests to remain with him. He even promises little, just in order to persuade them that it won't be any trouble.

Soon Abraham is providing a lavish meal for his guests, personally selecting choice animals from his herd. A man of Abraham's wealth could have allowed his servants to do all the preparations; however, Scripture demonstrates the personal involvement of Abraham and Sarah in this display of hospitality (18:6–8).

Abraham, Caring Family Member

Abraham's concern for family extends beyond his immediate relatives. Scripture details the relationship that Abraham maintained with Lot, his brother Haran's son. Although Haran died while still in Ur (11:28), Abraham cared for Lot throughout his stay in Mesopotamia, the journey into the land of Canaan and their sojourn in Egypt.

As Lot struggled through many trials leading to his capture during the war between the kings (Genesis 14), Abraham remained in close contact with his nephew, receiving word of Lot's capture. Abraham did not stand idly by but moved into action, saving his nephew, possessions, women and others. He did not abandon his nephew but restored him to the evil city in accordance with Lot's choice.

Further, when God announces His intent to destroy the cities of the plain, Abraham knows that Lot and his family are still there, awaiting the impending disaster about to befall them. It is no coincidence that the angels who are sent to destroy are also involved in saving Lot, his wife and daughters.

Abraham, Lover of God, Father of God's People

During the war between the kings (Genesis 14), we find Abraham involved, especially when his nephew was taken captive. Abraham maintained a large number of fighters and used strategy to defeat the enemy and rescue his family members held captive.

God's love and respect of Abraham are such that God questions, "Shall I hide from Abraham what I am about to do?" (18:17) Abraham's relationship to God is so close that he is later referred to as God's lover. Abraham here is quite bold. He is respectful of God but holds God to the standards expected of a righteous judge: "Will not the Judge of all the earth do right?" (18:25)

Perhaps the most outstanding example of the character of Abraham is his pleading with God for the sake of the inhabitants of Sodom and Gomorrah (18:23–32). Abraham plays upon God's attribute of mercy by mentioning God's sense of righteousness, that He would never sweep away the righteous with the wicked. In the true fashion of the Middle Eastern bazaar, Abraham bargains with God: "What if there be fifty righteous people in the city? Will you really sweep it away and spare the place for the sake of the fifty righteous people in it?" (18:24) He bargains God down to 45, 40, 30, 20, and 10. Finally, we see that the depravity of the cities is so great that even ten righteous people could not be found.

This episode typifies the difference between the character of Abraham and that of all who came before him. Even the truly righteous attested to in the Bible, such as Noah who was mentioned as a "...righteous man, blameless among the people of his time, and he walked with God" (6:9), displayed human weakness. When hearing that the entire world will be drowned in the

Flood, Noah is satisfied with the knowledge that he, his wife, his three sons and their wives will be saved in the ark. Nowhere is there mentioned even one word of protest by Noah. Noah is content to bask in the glory of his own righteousness.

But is it conceivable to envision Abraham allowing God to proceed with a destruction of all life, without a good fight? This shows the uniqueness of Abraham as the father of God's people.

Abraham's Self–Reliance

Following the rescue of Lot and the war of the kings, Abraham encountered King Melchizedek of Salem (14:18–24). Here we see Abraham's reliance on the King of the universe instead of the king of Salem. It is usual in war to take booty and captives. Melchizedek wants to take the people and offers Abraham the booty or possessions. Abraham reminds Melchizedek of his solemn oath: "I will accept nothing belonging to you, not even a thread or the thong of a sandal, so that you will never be able to say, 'I made Abram rich.'" (14:23). Abraham is reinforcing the value of independent achievement. Abraham makes it clear that his reliance is not on others, only on the Creator of heaven and earth.

Abraham's Covenant with God

Abraham, while believing in self–reliance to attain wealth and possessions, knows that offspring are a blessing from the Almighty. God appears to Abraham in a vision with a reassurance, "…Do not be afraid, Abram. I am your shield, your very great reward" (15:1). Not afraid to challenge God as to His sense of justice, Abraham confronts God: "…O sovereign Lord, what can you give me since I remain childless?" (15:2)

Abraham receives God's assurance: "…Look up at the heavens and count the stars—if indeed you can count them…so shall your offspring be" (15:5). The patriarchs and matriarchs of Israel are often barren (cf. Isaac and Rebecca, Leah and Rachel), infertile or unloved for long periods. Abraham, while having great faith in divine assurances, realizes that there are physical limits, due to the aging process. Since Sarah is infertile and old, and Abraham is 86 years old, it appears impossible to give birth. Sarah offers Hagar, her Egyptian maid servant, to lie with Abraham (Genesis 16). Although an offspring is produced, Ishmael will not become the true heir of Abraham's convenantal line.

Thirteen additional years pass after the birth of Ishmael. Sarah is now 90 and Abraham 99. These years have not succeeded in producing a genuine heir. Apparently the promise of numerous offspring cannot be fulfilled. Somehow, miraculously, Sarah and Abraham must give birth to a son in their old age. Their offspring, Isaac, will be a vital link in the chain, leading to the formation of a "kingdom of priests and a holy nation" (Exodus 19:6).

SCRIPTURE FOCUS

GENESIS 12:1 Now the Lord had said unto Abram, Get thee out of thy country, and from thy kindred, and from thy father's house, unto a land that I will show thee:

2 And I will make of thee a great nation, and I will bless thee, and make thy name great; and thou shalt be a blessing:

3 And I will bless them that bless thee, and curse him that curseth thee: and in thee shall all families of the earth be blessed.

4 So Abram departed, as the Lord had spoken unto him; and Lot went with him: and Abram was seventy and five years old when he departed out of Haran.

5 And Abram took Sarai his wife, and Lot his brother's son, and all their substance that they had gathered, and the souls that they had gotten in Haran; and they went forth to go into the land of Canaan; and into the land of Canaan they came.

6 And Abram passed through the land unto the place of Sichem, unto the plain of Moreh. And the Canaanite was then in the land.

7 And the Lord appeared unto Abram, and said, Unto thy seed will I give this land: and there builded he an altar unto the Lord, who appeared unto him.

8 And he removed from thence unto a mountain on the east of Beth–el, and pitched his tent, having Beth–el on the west, and Hai on the east: and there he builded an altar unto the Lord, and called upon the name of the Lord.

HEBREWS 11:8 By faith Abraham, when he was called to go out into a place which he should after receive for an inheritance, obeyed; and he went out, not knowing whither he went.

9 By faith he sojourned in the land of promise, as in a strange country, dwelling in tabernacles with Isaac and Jacob, the heirs with him of the same promise:

10 For he looked for a city which hath foundations, whose builder and maker is God.

11 Through faith also Sarah herself received strength to conceive seed, and was delivered of a child when she was past age, because she judged him faithful who had promised.

12 Therefore sprang there even of one, and him as good as dead, so many as the stars of the sky in multitude, and as the sand which is by the seashore innumerable.

SCRIPTURE SEARCH

Write T (for True) or F (for False) at the end of each sentence.

1. Abraham was from a family that worshiped idol gods.____
2. Abraham was born in Jerusalem. ____
3. Abraham's wife was Ruth.____
4. Abraham preparing to sacrifice his son is called the "binding of Isaac."____
5. Abraham was a man of faith, compassion and hope.____

The African American Connection

1. Strong Role Models

Throughout American history, African Americans have had strong role models. Crispus Attucks, Frederick Douglass, Mary McLeod Bethune, Madame C. J. Walker and Benjamin Mays are a few names that come to mind. But no society or group within a society has ever had enough strong role models.

Abraham certainly qualifies as an outstanding role model with strong African ties. He often lived in hostile environments but refused to allow these places and circumstances to obliterate his faith in God. The United States is not a friendly land to African Americans. But like Abraham and many of our other ancestors, we will continue to survive, struggle and succeed.

2. Our Own Rhythm

In a world of conformity, Abraham was a nonconformist. The trends in his society would dictate that he follow the prudent path of silence. Abraham was never silent. He saw clearly the correct path in life, and he taught his family the right way. He raised a family that carried his name with dignity. No longer would anyone conceive of him or his people as idol worshipers. Abraham's name became synonymous with faith, dignity, strength, wealth and blessing.

Is it by mistake that we are here in America? Should we become one more ingredient in the American "soup" or does God have a specific purpose for us here? Has God called us, like He did Abraham? How can we best seek God's individual and collective will?

3. Scars and Stars

Along with American Indians and the Jews of Germany during World War II, undoubtedly African Americans have been victimized and persecuted. Abraham's ability to overcome obstacles is refreshing in a world where casting blame on others for our present conditions often seems the order of the day. Booker T. Washington began life as a slave but rose up from slavery to become an adviser to presidents. Abraham was a man of humble birth. He came from a family that did not believe in Jehovah. But by God's grace and much hard work he became a man of tremendous material wealth and enough spiritual riches to share with all the world.

4. What Do You Think?

A. Should we be asked or expected to forget our victimization?

B. Can we allow our wounds to stop us from achieving excellence?

C. Can we allow our yesterdays to shackle our todays and tomorrows?

D. Can we permit ourselves to become permanently dependent upon our former enslavers?

E. What principle from Abraham's life applies to African American families today?

CHAPTER FIVE

LET MY PEOPLE GO!

Let's Discover . . .

Can God use a senior citizen to overthrow a powerful nation, to rescue His people from slavery, to show His love for oppressed people?
Let's discover how God uses an older person to lead His people into freedom, abundance and joy!

MOSES:
Let My People Go!

Rabbi Sanford H. Shudnow
Exodus 2:1-10; Hebrews 11:24-29

Moses: The Man

Moses or *Moshe* in the Hebrew, is perhaps the most famous person in the Old Testament. Pharaoh's daughter called him *Moshe* meaning: "I bore him from the water" (Exodus 2:10).

Moses: Birth and Background

Many biblical verses are devoted to Moses and the circumstances of his birth, quite unlike Abraham's whose birth is a mystery. We know many of the particulars leading up to Moses's birth, because they set the stage for the miraculous role of leadership he plays in the redemption of God's nation from slavery to freedom.

The conditions of the Israelite nation a generation prior to Moses's birth were ideal. Although the people originally arrived in Egypt from Canaan due to the seven–year famine, they were treated as royalty. They enjoyed a cordial welcome from Pharaoh and his assistant, their brother, Joseph. But while all seemed favorable, circumstances deteriorated rapidly under a new king. The Scripture states: "A new king, who did not know of Joseph, arose over Egypt" (1:8).

There is much disagreement among scholars as to the date and identity of the new king. Apparently he was Thutmose IV, who lived in the 15th century B.C.[1] The people of God were oppressed, enslaved and remained in exile for 400 years as was foretold to Abraham (Genesis 15:13).

56

As the oppression and enslavement increased, so too did the seeming impossibility of the birth of a redeemer. According to Pharaoh's decree, the male children were to be cast into the Nile while the girls were allowed to live (Exodus 1:22).

To circumvent Pharaoh's orders, Moses's parents concealed him for a period of three months, and then placed him in a basket in the bulrushes of the Nile. Much here is of significance, including the fact that the Nile is revered by the ancient Egyptians as a god, also that the same word for "basket" *tey–vah* is employed in the Flood story for Noah's "ark." Just as the ark saved remnants of all world civilizations and is guided only by the hand of God, so too the destiny of God's people is directed by His hand.

Moses is drawn from the water and adopted by Pharaoh's daughter. Moses's sister Miriam offers to find a nursemaid for her brother. She proposes to Pharaoh's daughter none other than Jocheved, Moses's own mother. Thus Moses is reared by his mother in the palace of Pharaoh with all of the splendor and privilege accompanying that status.

The oppression increases. God hears the cries of His people and sets into motion the forces leading to their redemption. The theme of redemption is a constant throughout Scripture.

Years later, for the first time as a mature adult, Moses witnesses the oppression of his own people, the Hebrews. The shocking sight of an Egyptian taskmaster beating a Hebrew slave is too much for him. He reacts, killing the Egyptian (Exodus 2:11–12).

Knowing the severity of punishment due him, he flees to the land of Midian, where he marries Zipporah, Jethro's daughter, a woman of African descent.

Moses: Nation Builder

In Midian, the desert of Sinai, Moses encounters God at a burning bush, where he accepts the charge by God to be the vehicle of God's deliverance of His people. For the first time, Moses meets with his brother Aaron, who ultimately becomes Moses's right hand man and the high priest of Israel. The two appear before Pharaoh and his court, performing various signs and miracles in order to demonstrate that they are the chosen by God Almighty to act as His agents (7:8–12).

God sends a series of ten plagues, reaching a crescendo in the slaying of the firstborn of the Egyptians, by the hand of the Angel of Death (7:17–21; 8:1–6, 16–17, 20–22; 9:6, 8 –11, 22–25; 10:12–15, 21–23; 11:4–8). Each plague is an opportunity for Pharaoh to relent and release the slaves, but he remains obstinate.

The killing of the firstborn in Egypt is the supreme test of Pharaoh's resistance to Moses and God. Pharaoh finally gives in, releasing the slaves, but not without a good chase culminating in his own destruction (Exodus 14). Moses finds himself at the Sea of Crossing, the Red Sea, surrounded on all sides by the enemy. God performs the miracle of splitting the sea, allowing the Israelites to pass through the sea on dry ground. No sooner do they pass through, then the waters engulf Pharaoh and his Egyptian charioteers.

From this point Moses must deal with the nation of Israel and their needs and complaints. Throughout their 40 years of wandering in the wilderness of Sinai, they complain of lack of water, bread and meat. Moses is sympathetic, but it is God who miraculously provides for their needs. Perhaps the greatest event during the trek through the desert takes place at Mount Sinai, where Moses ascends the mountain, receiving the two tablets of stone engraved with the Ten Commandments (Exodus 19—20). Moses then communicates God's law to Israel, and becomes known as the lawgiver and judge.

Moses takes charge of the structure of the nation and their military campaigns and marches in the desert. During this time Moses chooses Bezalel and other skilled craftsmen for the construction of the Tabernacle, to house the Ark of the Witness or Covenant. This Tabernacle becomes the physical testimony to God's presence within the Israelite camp.

At the close of the 40–year period, while standing across the Jordan River, Moses speaks to the nation in a series of farewell addresses, recorded in the Book of Deuteronomy. He charges his people and places them into the hands of Joshua, the new leader. Moses then dies on the mountain, having viewed the land from afar. He is buried by God in an unknown grave, at the ripe old age of 120.

Moses: God's Humble Servant

Moses may justly be considered the greatest prophet in Israel, as Jewish tradition assigns to him the title *Avi Ha–Neviim*—"The Father of Prophets," and their greatest teacher, *Moshe Rabeinu,* "Moses Our Teacher." Yet he was known for his modesty. The title given him in Scripture is *Moshe Av–dee*—"Moses My Servant."

In his august status as senior prophet, teacher, leader and priest, Moses is truly noteworthy because he assumes the role of humble servant to both God and humankind, and he does it so well. Moses never ascribes to himself any special role or powers. At the burning bush (Exodus 3), Moses responds to God by asking, "Who am I, that I should go to Pharaoh and bring the Israelites out of Egypt?" (Exodus 3:11) In a last ditch effort, he tries to convince God of his unsuitability to lead by complaining, "O Lord, I have never been eloquent…I am slow of speech and tongue…O Lord, please send someone else to do it" (Exodus 4:10, 13).

Moses's humility is shown also when his sister Miriam slanders him and becomes leprous. Instead of cursing her and attacking her, Moses prays for her healing: "…O God, please heal her!" (Numbers 12:13) No time was to be wasted in helping even those who slandered him.

Moses: Man of Justice and Balance

As Moses proceeds from his Egyptian identity to an Israelite one, he never loses his sense of balance. No sooner does he witness an injustice against one of his people, than he witnesses the injustice of an Israelite to his fellow Israelite. He asks the Israelite, "Why are you beating your brother?" (Exodus 2:13) The coarse response: "Who made you prince and judge over us? Do you mean to kill me as you did the Egyptian?" (2:14) This causes fear in Moses's heart because of possible retribution for his killing of the Egyptian taskmaster.

This episode demonstrates a point in the evolution of Moses as a leader. He is full of inner conflict, yet knows what is right and wrong, whether done by an Egyptian or an Israelite. It may have taken some time before Moses learned to develop balance, but his sense of right and wrong was always acute.

Moses: Compassionate Shepherd

Moses fled for his life to Midian from the reach of Pharaoh. His experience at the well, where his destined bride, Zipporah and her sisters were bothered by other shepherds, shows his bravery and compassion. The scene at the well reminds us of the method by which Rebecca and Rachel are chosen for Isaac and Jacob. Moses was fearless in his defense of the helpless maidens and then drew the water for them to water their flock. Later in Scripture, care for the stranger becomes a principle and theme: "When an alien lives with you in your land, do not mistreat him. The alien living with you must be treated as one of your native–born. Love him as yourself, for you were aliens in Egypt. I am the Lord your God" (Leviticus 19:33–34).

The experience in Egypt was the setting and proving ground for Moses's leadership role. His sojourn away from his people with Ruel or Jethro, the priest of Midian, set the stage for later involvement with Jethro in the development of his leadership style.

Moses: Man of Respect

A. Moses Respects Jethro. Upon meeting Jethro, Moses shows tremendous love, affection and respect for his father–in–law. Scripture relates, "So Moses went out to meet his father–in–law and bowed down and kissed him. They greeted each other and then went into the tent. Moses told his father–in–law about everything the Lord had done to Pharaoh and the Egyptians for Israel's sake..." (Exodus 18:7–8). This interaction between Moses and Jethro is interesting and unprecedented in his relationship with any other person. Jethro is seen to be, at least in the eyes of Scripture, a righteous Gentile. Nowhere does Moses greet even Aaron, his brother, with such respect and affection. Jethro was a man of great wisdom who commanded Moses's utmost respect and reverence.

B. Moses Respects the Property of Others. In ancient times, a leader's respect for the property of his subjects was unheard of. Rulers routinely confiscated property. This applied not only to real estate and chattels, but also to family members, servants and even the subjects' brides.

Moses went to great lengths to avoid even the appearance of improper behavior. His impeccable behavior is evidenced when Moses endured the most significant challenge to his authority during the rebellion of Korah and his 250 followers. The only complaint they could register against Moses was his office of leadership, when ideally all of Israel "deserved" a position of leadership. Korah and his followers' opposition to Moses and Aaron was a poorly guised coup. They said, "You have gone too far! The whole community is holy, every one of them, and the Lord is with them. Why then do you set yourselves above the Lord's assembly?" (Numbers 16:3)

Moses answered the challenge to his leadership by reaffirming his commissioning by God. Moses left the resolution of this matter to God's divine intervention. His own non–intervention demonstrated his selection by God and affirmed Moses's sense of propriety.

Moses: The Team Leader

Nepotism, the appointment of family members to positions of prominence, is totally lacking in Moses's leadership. At first blush the appointment of Aaron, his brother, as high priest, seemed to be a supreme case of nepotism. But when God first approaches Moses at the burning bush (Exodus 3) with His request that Moses appear before Pharaoh and lead the Israelites out of slavery, it is God who appoints Aaron as Moses's second in charge. Speaking of Aaron God says, "...I know he can speak well...He will speak to the people for you, and it will be as if he were your mouth and as if you were God to him" (Exodus 4:14, 16).

Moses and Aaron work together, both as a team and separately, as required. But when it comes to the succession of leadership, Aaron's priestly line continues on to this day, while Moses's office ceased with his death. His two sons, Gershom and Eliezer (Exodus 18:3–4) are but names in Scripture, all but disregarded. The same is true of Zipporah, his wife.

Moses's chosen successor is Joshua, the son of Nun, originally named Hoshea (Numbers 13:16). Joshua came from the tribe of Ephraim, differing from that of Moses, who was from the tribe of Levi. If Moses desired to practice nepotism, he could have easily chosen one of his clansmen. He did not. He chose the best person for the job.

Moses: Learning How to Delegate

Moses was chastised by his father–in–law, Jethro, for being too much of a work horse; in today's terms, a workaholic.

When Jethro witnessed Moses in his capacity as judge (Exodus 18:13), he was greatly troubled by what he saw. Moses alone judged the people, causing them to stand around idle from morning until evening. Witnessing the needless delay caused in attending to cases, Jethro offers sound advice: "Select capable men from all the people—men who fear God, trustworthy men who hate dishonest gain—and appoint them as officials over thousands, hundreds, fifties and tens...but have them bring every difficult case to you; the simple cases they can decide themselves" (Exodus 18:21–22). Moses immediately acts upon this advice. He was not intimidated in any way by the counsel of someone who was a non–Israelite. The principle of delegation of authority became the standard for administration, on the tribal and national level.

Moses: Man of Prayer

There are many Scripture references to Moses as a man of prayer. He prays on behalf of his people when he hears of their travail and sufferings, when Pharaoh refused to provide straw to the slaves for brick making.

Moses prayed for the Egyptians as well. On several occasions, when the suffering of the Egyptians leading to the Exodus was approaching its climax, Moses and Aaron are called by Pharaoh to pray.

Later, in Exodus 32, when the Israelites commit the sin of worshiping the golden calf, Moses prays for them. God threatened to exterminate them and make a new nation of Moses himself. Moses chastised the people for their sins, and then returned to God and prayed: "...Oh, what a great sin these people have committed! They have made themselves gods of gold. But now, please forgive their sin—but if not, then blot me out of the book you have written" (Exodus 32:31–32).

Moses: Servant of People

Moses was 80 years old when he appeared before Pharaoh (Exodus 7:7). He served his people until his death 40 years later at age 120. While Moses served as leader of the nation, the people demonstrated dissatisfaction with their living conditions in the Sinai desert. They complained to him for water and meat, forgetting and exaggerating the conditions and advantages of Egypt. The people grew impatient with Moses when he remained on Mount Sinai for 40 days, receiving the first tablets of the covenant. They rebelled against his leadership, as in the uprising of Korah. Still Moses remained the undisputed champion of his people.

Because the nation exhibited lack of faith when Moses sent out 12 spies to explore the Promised Land, Israel wandered in the wilderness of Sinai for 40 years (Numbers 13—14). The generation that had experienced God's miracles and wonders in Egypt died in the desert and a new generation arose to enter the new land (Numbers 14:23). Nonetheless, while knowing that he and that generation would not live to inherit the land, Moses remained faithful to the dream, nurturing a new generation.

Moses: Man of God

It would be natural to assume that Moses, who had undergone so much during his long life, would have gone to great lengths to let his fame be known. He was destined for greatness by virtue of his Levitical birth and adoption by Pharaoh's daughter. He was chosen by God, standing before Pharaoh and his court performing signs and wonders, receiving and transmitting God's word to the people, judging them and leading them for 40 years. Yet his modesty was his most significant attribute.

Moses knew he was powerless to execute any wonder or miracle; God was always in charge. At the greatest of moments, the splitting of the Red Sea, Moses holds out his staff and says reassuringly, "Do not be afraid. Stand firm and you will see the deliverance the Lord will bring you today...The Lord will fight for you; you need only to be still" (Exodus 14:13–14).

Moses purposely took a back seat to God, the One who truly executes miracles. Yet almost against his will Moses received honor along with God. Scripture states, "And when the Israelites saw the great power the Lord displayed against the Egyptians, the people feared the Lord and put their trust in him and in Moses his servant" (Exodus 14:31).

Moses is but the strongest link in a long chain of those who lead God's people. Moses transferred the reigns of leadership to Joshua and the next generation. No one knew of his burial place. Grieved by the nation and forever remembered, Moses was not venerated as a god. His grave, perhaps purposely unknown, never became an object of worship. The Bible thereby emphasizes the transient status of leadership. Moses served his purpose as a leader and then passed on. Moses and all who would succeed him are charged with serving God and His people by doing God's will.

SCRIPTURE FOCUS

EXODUS 2:1 And there went a man of the house of Levi, and took to wife a daughter of Levi.

2 And the woman conceived, and bare a son: and when she saw him that he was a goodly child, she hid him three months.

3 And when she could not longer hide him, she took for him an ark of bulrushes, and daubed it with slime and with pitch, and put the child therein; and she laid it in the flags by the river's brink.

4 And his sister stood afar off, to wit what would be done to him.

5 And the daughter of Pharaoh came down to wash herself at the river; and her maidens walked along by the river's side; and when she saw the ark among the flags, she sent her maid to fetch it.

6 And when she had opened it, she saw the child: and, behold, the babe wept. And she had compassion on him, and said, This is one of the Hebrews' children.

7 Then said his sister to Pharaoh's daughter, Shall I go and call to thee a nurse of the Hebrew women, that she may nurse the child for thee?

8 And Pharaoh's daughter said to her, Go. And the maid went and called the child's mother.

9 And Pharaoh's daughter said unto her, Take this child away, and nurse it for me, and I will

65

give thee thy wages. And the woman took the child, and nursed it.

10 And the child grew, and she brought him unto Pharaoh's daughter, and he became her son. And she called his name Moses: and she said, Because I drew him out of the water.

HEBREWS 11:24 By faith Moses, when he was come to years, refused to be called the son of Pharaoh's daughter;

25 Choosing rather to suffer affliction with the people of God, than to enjoy the pleasures of sin for a season;

26 Esteeming the reproach of Christ greater riches than the treasures in Egypt: for he had respect unto the recompense of the reward.

27 By faith he forsook Egypt, not fearing the wrath of the king: for he endured, as seeing him who is invisible.

28 Through faith he kept the passover, and the sprinkling of blood, lest he that destroyed the firstborn should touch them.

29 By faith they passed through the Red sea as by dry land: which the Egyptians assaying to do were drowned.

SCRIPTURE SEARCH

Fill in the blanks.

1. God used Moses to rescue the Hebrews from slavery in

_____.

2. Moses's name means "I bore or drew him from the

_____."

3. Moses was raised by his _____ and Pharaoh's

_____.

4. Moses's mother was _____, his wife was _____, his brother was _____ and his father–in–law was _____.

5. Moses was a man of _____ service, of justice and _____, compassion, and respect and _____. But most of all, he was a man of _____.

The African American Connection

1. Conflicts

Because we pattern our lives after Christ, is it possible that we may often overlook the richness and variety of human qualities of Old Testament characters? Our imaginations are charged by some of the images of Moses, especially baby Moses in the bulrushes, the scene at the Red Sea or with the two tablets in hand at Mount Sinai. But how many think of Moses as a man steeped in two diametrically opposing cultures and having to make a choice? He was born into the elitist class of the Hebrews, but was raised in the palace of the king of Egypt. How many think of Moses as a person who experienced conflict between his immediate family and his job as leader of a nation?

2. Dream Keepers

Moses never lived to see the fulfillment of his mission. But he died with the knowledge that he had helped to forge a new nation, nurture a new leadership, and give strength to a new and vital generation that did not experience the degradations of enslavement. He set into motion the organization and structure of a new society in a new land.

Dr. Martin Luther King, Jr. alluded to Moses's experience in a speech the night before his assassination. He said, "I've been to the mountaintop...I've seen the Promised Land...I may not get there...but we as a people will get to the Promised Land."

3. What Do You Think?

A. What are some parallels between the conflicts in Moses's life and the conflicts in our lives?

B. Give two examples of how Moses's humility increased his effectiveness as a leader, and name two African American leaders, contemporary or from history, who can be said to be humble. Then give two advantages and two disadvantages of being known as a humble leader. Was Jesus a humble leader? See Philippians 2:5–11.

C. As African American Christians, do we have any responsibility to help keep alive the dream of full social, political and economic freedom for all citizens of the United States, and for all citizens of the world?

D. What are three important ways that your church can help "keep the dream alive" and work for its fulfillment?

E. In what ways are Moses's dreams of a promised land, Dr. King's dream of a world free from racism, poverty and war, and Jesus' dream of the kingdom of God alike?

CHAPTER SIX

SISTER, TAKE CHARGE!

LET'S DISCOVER . . .

Can God use a woman to lead men? To win victories? To bring peace? Let's discover how God uses teamwork to bring about spiritual and social change!

DEBORAH:
Sister, Take Charge!

Chaplain Melody L.H. Goodwin
Judges 4:1-10, 14-15; 5:1-3

Deborah was Israel's only woman judge.[1] Her story is found in Judges, chapters four and five. We do not know her genealogy, when or where she was born, and there is no record of where she died. We do know that she was married to Lapidoth and lived between Bethel and Ramah in the hill country of Ephraim (Judges 4:4–5).

Deborah's name means "bee" and Lapidoth's name means "torches" or "lightning flashes." It has been suggested that Deborah would never have become such a dazzling figure in biblical history were it not for the love, sympathy, advice and encouragement of a husband who was happy to ride in the "second chariot."[2]

Deborah was also a prophetess, agitator, poetess and maternal figure in Israel.[3] Because of Deborah's dedication, God allowed her to judge Israel for 40 years (Judges 5:31).

Deborah is important to us because she represents what God can do through a woman who submits herself to God's will. Let's study Deborah's life to see the heroic part she played in delivering God's people.

Deborah: Woman of Many Roles
Deborah was a ruler, the fifth judge. All of Israel was her jurisdiction. Deborah's responsibility as a judge was to hear and decide cases. Biblical judges were chosen by God and made their decisions based on the laws of God.

70

Periodically the Children of Israel needed to be delivered from bondage caused by their worship of idol gods. In addition to hearing and deciding cases, the judges' responsibilities were to protect Israel from attack and do battle when enemies were to be subdued. As a result of Deborah's leadership, Israel enjoyed justice and peace.

Deborah was a prophetess. A prophetess is a female who speaks for God and interprets events in light of God's words and works.[4] Deborah had to be able to discern the purposes of God and declare them to others. In Bible days prophets and prophetesses were mediators between God and His people. They were divinely inspired and correspond to some preachers and pastors of today.

In the Old Testament, only three women are said to have been prophetesses: Miriam, the sister of Moses (Exodus 15:20); Hulda, a woman who spoke in the time of Josiah (2 Kings 22:14–20) and Deborah (Judges 4 and 5). Deborah used her gift as political and judicial leader of the nation for the good of her people.

Deborah was an agitator. An agitator stirs up and excites public discussion with the view of producing change.[5] Deborah stirred up Israel's concern about its low spiritual condition. She aroused the nation from its lethargy and despair. She awoke in them a determination to free themselves from their situation of bondage and degradation.

As poetess, Deborah's contribution to history and literature appears in Judges 4 and 5 in two forms. The first is the prose of chapter 4 and the second is the poetry in chapter 5. The poetry is commonly known as the "Song of Deborah," a celebration of victory. The prose and poetry tell essentially the same story of two Israelite heroines—Deborah, who spurred the military leader Barak on to victory; and Jael, the wife of Heber the Kenite, who assassinated the fleeing enemy General Sisera.

Finally, in addition to all of these roles, Deborah was a wife to Lapidoth and mother to a nation that had turned its back on God.

With love, care, tenderness and toughness when needed, she was instrumental in helping Israel get right with God. We have no record of her having experienced actual motherhood, but Lockyer paints this beautiful picture of Deborah:

"The highest of all of her remarkable gifts was her trust in God which is ever the source of any woman's highest adornment. As she sat under her palm tree to rule in righteousness and translate the revelation of God, her heart was filled with grace divine which diffused itself like a sweet smelling savor over the whole land."[6]

Deborah: Woman of Action

Deborah was chosen and raised up by God to lead His people at a crucial time in their history. Jabin was king of the Canaanites. He reigned in Hazor and oppressed the Israelites for 20 years (4:3). Not much information is given on him personally, but he enlisted Sisera as commander of his army and used him as an instrument of oppression. Sisera lived in Harosheth Haggoyim and was the supervisor of Jabin's military forces.

One day while Deborah was deciding disputes, God revealed to her how to deliver the Israelites out of the hand of Sisera and the Canaanites. Deborah then sent for Barak, a military strategist, to come and organize the Israelites' military forces. Barak said that he would come and lead the military only if Deborah would agree to go with him into battle. Deborah agreed but gave Barak this warning:

"…because of the way you are going about this, the honor will not be yours, for the Lord will hand Sisera over to a woman" (4:9, NIV).

Deborah and Barak went to Kedesh, where he summoned the tribes of Zebulun and Naphtali. Barak organized 10,000 men to assist them in the battle. King Jabin summoned Sisera, also an outstanding military leader, to organize his military force. Sisera had 900 iron chariots and the men from Harosheth Haggoyim. Deborah gave the word, and Barak and his army charged Sisera's forces and killed them all, except Sisera (4:14–15).

Sisera escaped, abandoned his chariot and fled on foot. He ran to Jael, the wife of Heber the Kenite, because there was a friendly relationship between King Jabin and the Kenite clan. Jael heard Sisera coming, ran out to meet him and called him into her tent. Sisera went in, she covered him up and hid him. He asked her to stand in the tent entrance and told her if anyone came and asked if she had seen him, she was to say no. Sisera was so exhausted from running that he fell fast asleep. While he was asleep, Jael took a tent peg and drove it through his temple, killing him (4:21).

When Barak came in search of Sisera, Jael went out to meet him, and called him to see the man he was looking for. When he looked in he found Sisera dead.

That day God delivered the Israelites out of the hands of Jabin, and Jael was the woman Deborah was talking about when she prophesied to Barak, "God will deliver Sisera over to a woman" (4:9).

Barak is included among the judges who liberated Israel from her oppressors (1 Samuel 12:11), and he is mentioned in the New Testament catalogue of people who exercised great faith in God (Hebrews 11:32). Barak's courage resulted from the encouragement of Deborah, his spiritual mother, who is *not* mentioned in either 1 Samuel 12 or Hebrews 11.

Deborah: An Effective Leader

Dr. Bennie Goodwin has defined an effective leader as "a person who gets the right things done by the right people at the right time and place."[7]

As we examine Deborah's life as a judge of Israel, we discover that she is a good example of an effective leader. Deborah was faced with two problems, one spiritual and one military

(Judges 4:1–3). She handled the spiritual problem by motivating the people of Israel to turn back to God. She handled the military problem by finding the right person to organize their forces and lead them into a battle in which God gave them the victory (4:6–7, 16).

Deborah was a woman of constructive action. By God's revelation she determined what was right and proceeded to do it. She knew that in order to accomplish her goal she had to identify her problem and formulate her purposes.

Secondly, she chose the right person to work with her. She was aware of the problems and potential of the person she selected to help her. When it was time to go to battle, she was very realistic. She knew she had a military problem, therefore she needed someone with military experience to help her. She sent for Barak because he was known for his military expertise (4:15–16). Barak was a great battle organizer but was not good in leading the fight alone (4:8). Knowing this, she allowed him to organize the troops but assisted him in leading the troops into battle. She allowed him to do what he could do and she assisted him only when she was needed.

Finally, Deborah was a leader who spent her time and energy wisely. When God called her to be Israel's only woman judge, she made herself available and set about doing God's work. Does this imply that she prayed and practiced her religious convictions on a daily basis? How else could she be prepared to accept God's call and challenge? Deborah set herself apart from anything that would interfere with the effective carrying out of the task God had given her. Deborah situated herself in a place where the people had access to her and she judged them with wisdom and spiritual guidance as she was led by God. In Judges 4:5 (NIV) it is written:

> "And she held court under the palm of Deborah
> between Ramah and Bethel in the hill country of
> Ephraim, and the Israelites came to her to have
> their disputes settled."

SCRIPTURE FOCUS

JUDGES 4:1 And the children of Israel again did evil in the sight of the Lord, when Ehud was dead.

2 And the Lord sold them into the hand of Jabin king of Canaan, that reigned in Hazor; the captain of whose host was Sisera, which dwelt in Harosheth of the Gentiles.

3 And the children of Israel cried unto the Lord: for he had nine hundred chariots of iron; and twenty years he mightily oppressed the children of Israel.

4 And Deborah, a prophetess, the wife of Lapidoth, she judged Israel at that time.

5 And she dwelt under the palm tree of Deborah, between Ramah and Beth–el in mount Ephraim: and the children of Israel came up to her for judgment.

6 And she sent and called Barak the son of Abinoam out of Kedesh-naphtali, and said unto him, Hath not the Lord God of Israel commanded, saying, Go and draw toward mount Tabor, and take with thee ten thousand men of the children of Naphtali and of the children of Zebulun?

7 And I will draw unto thee to the river Kishon Sisera, the captain of Jabin's army, with his chariots and his multitude; and I will deliver him into thine hand.

8 And Barak said unto her, If thou wilt go with me, then I will go: but if thou wilt not go with me, then I will not go.

9 And she said, I will surely go with thee: not-

75

withstanding the journey that thou takest shall not be for thine honour; for the Lord shall sell Sisera into the hand of a woman. And Deborah arose, and went with Barak to Kedesh.

10 And Barak called Zebulun and Naphtali to Kedesh; and he went up with ten thousand men at his feet: and Deborah went up with him.

14 And Deborah said unto Barak, Up; for this is the day in which the Lord hath delivered Sisera into thine hand: is not the Lord gone out before thee? So Barak went down from mount Tabor, and ten thousand men after him.

15 And the Lord discomfited Sisera, and all his chariots, and all his host, with the edge of the sword before Barak; so that Sisera lighted down off his chariot, and fled away on his feet.

JUDGES 5:1 Then sang Deborah and Barak the son of Abinoam on that day, saying,

2 Praise ye the Lord for the avenging of Israel, when the people willingly offered themselves.

3 Hear, O ye kings; give ear, O ye princes; I, even I, will sing unto the Lord; I will sing praise to the Lord God of Israel.

SCRIPTURE SEARCH

Let's play "Bible Jeopardy." Here are the answers. What are the questions?

1. *Lapidoth.* Who was Deborah's _____?
2. *Judge.* Who were persons who led the _____ between the time of Joshua and _____, the first king?

3. *Barak.* Who led Deborah's _____?
4. *Effective leaders.* Who are persons who get the _____ things done through _____ people at the _____ time and place?
5. *Deborah.* Who was a woman of many gifts: a r_____, j_____, prophetess, agitator, p_____, w_____, mother and woman of a_____?

The African American Connection

There are some lessons we can learn from Deborah's life that can help us with the issues and problems of the African American church and community.

1. Use Our Resources

First we must use what we have to help deliver ourselves from our oppression. Deborah had God–given gifts, talents and a special ability to find the people she needed and give them the resources and support they needed. We have persons in our community through whom God can solve problems that plague us. What they need is our spiritual, moral and financial support. The Civil Rights Movement of the 1950s and '60s proved what God can do through us when we use what we have among us, for our own deliverance.

2. Become Agitators

Secondly, we can become agitators. African Americans have a history of allowing one person to be our leader, and that person has spoken on our behalf to the ruling political party. Leaders such as Martin Luther King, Jr. and more recently Reverend Jesse Jackson have been agitators on our behalf. Isn't it time for all African Americans to become

agitators? Hasn't the time come for all of us to stir up and ex-
cite public discussion with the view of producing positive
changes?

3. Initiate Liberation

Thirdly, we must initiate our own liberation. Doesn't
Deborah's experience affirm our own? The oppressor will
continue to oppress us until we decide not to allow it. The
Children of Israel remained oppressed by King Jabin, until
someone stepped in to be the link between their situation and
God's ability to deliver them. Isn't God always available to
deliver us when we make ourselves available to Him?
Deborah was the link between the Israelites' oppressive situation and God's ability to deliver them. Deborah pushed God's
oppressed people toward freedom.

Sometimes freedom has to be gained on the battlefield. Our
battlefields today are: joblessness, homelessness, drug abuse,
teen pregnancies, hunger, alcoholism, incest, incarceration of
young Black males, lack of family unity and lack of spiritual
commitment. These and other problems are at epidemic levels
in the Black community. Are any of these social problems our
own responsibility? Are some caused by social injustices at
the local, state, or federal government level?

In the book, *Straight from the Heart,* Jesse Jackson made
this point:

> "While I know that the victimizers may be
> responsible for the victims being down, the vic-
> tim must be responsible...for initiating change,
> determining strategy, tactics, timing and being
> disciplined enough to pull it off. No one has a
> greater self–interest than the victims in getting
> up, while the victimizers do not perceive it to be
> in their self–interest."[8]

Jesse Jackson calls African Americans, along with other minorities, "the rejected stones." He suggests that it will be these "rejected stones" that will form the cornerstone of the nation. He believes that those rejected by society because of race, gender or economic situation, have a special role in bringing about social change.[9] Can we deliver our people by becoming the links that bring about change in our community? Are we willing to make ourselves available to our community, spiritually and politically?

4. Trust God

A final lesson we can learn from Deborah is the benefits of listening to and putting our trust in God. Deborah's actions were ordered and ordained by God. Our challenge is to do what Deborah and Jesus did. They were both sent to deliver God's people. They had "marching orders" from God. To help deliver our people from the destructive course we're on, our "marching orders" should be the same as theirs. Deborah's are recorded in Judges 4:6 (NIV):

"The Lord, the God of Israel commands you:
'Go, take with you ten thousand men of Naphtali
and Zebulun and lead the way to Mount Tabor.'"

Jesus' "marching orders" are recorded in Luke 4:18 (NIV):
"The Spirit of the Lord is on me, because he has
anointed me to preach good news to the poor. He
sent me to proclaim freedom for the prisoners
and recovery of sight for the blind, to release the
oppressed, to proclaim the year of the Lord's
favor."

"Marching orders" are dictated by the social and spiritual problems plaguing God's people during a particular era. The problems in the African American community are many. Our brothers and sisters are in danger. Our challenge is to declare war on these problems and seek to wipe them out. Do we need to be in a place where it is easier to hear God's instructions on how we are to minister to the needs of our community? Is the church such a place? Once we have received our "marching orders" from God, can we trust Him to be faithful to His Word in assisting us with our assignment?

God can be trusted to do His part, but we must do ours.

5. What Do You Think?

There are some very practical ways that we can help each other. Tutorial programs, visiting prisoners, food programs, child care programs, mental health counseling and community Bible studies are a few.

A. Can you think of other ways you can help people?

B. In what community ministries is your church engaged?

C. What ministries does your church need to add?

D. How can your church improve the community ministries in which it is engaged?

E. What are some ways that Christian love can be exhibited?

CHAPTER SEVEN

THE MAN IN THE MIDDLE

LET's DISCOVER . . .

Can God use a mother's prayer to provide a leader? To link a nation's dawn to its noonday?
Let's discover how God can use one committed person to move a large group toward its appointed destiny.

SAMUEL:
The Man in the Middle

Minister Mark Jeffers
1 Samuel 1:9-11, 20, 24-28; 3:1-10

If one word can be used to summarize the life of Samuel that word would be "consecrated." Even before his birth, this man was set apart by his mother for special training in the ministry of the Lord. He grew up living with the high priest of Israel, committing his ways to the service of God. When the time came for young Samuel to minister, God raised him to national prominence as Israel's judge and gave him prophetic words of revelation. As priest, he led the people of God into revival. As the final judge of Israel, Samuel anointed both King Saul and David.

Samuel demonstrates the importance of consecrating our lives to God. He was placed in the midst of a people who had been led astray. He took the reigns of spiritual leadership and brought them back to God.

Who Was Samuel?
He was the first child born to a woman who had been barren much of her marriage. Samuel was special to Hannah and was raised in the tabernacle where he learned the duties of a priest.

He became the first prophet to speak after a long time of silence from God. Israel had become spiritually weak and corrupt, so Samuel's prophetic voice marked the beginning of a turn–around for the nation. When God chose him to be His prophet, Samuel was submissive and reverent to God's word and will. Soon afterward Eli, the high priest and Samuel's mentor died, so Samuel naturally filled the vacancy and became Israel's new spiritual leader.

As his ministry unfolded, Samuel became a judge over Israel. A judge was like a spiritual monitor of the people, who settled their disputes and often led them out of rebellion into repentance. The judge brought the nation (or sometimes just a few tribes) out of the oppression that God had put them under because of their rebellious hearts. As judge, Samuel was righteous, honest, and sensitive to the people's needs. The office also required him to be an administrator and organizer, since he was responsible for the maintenance of the nation's spiritual purity. Samuel was the only individual in Israel's history to be prophet, priest, and judge.

Samuel's Mother, Hannah

In Shiloh lived the high priest and his company of ordained men. In their hands was the awesome responsibility of keeping the sacred possessions of their nation—the tabernacle, the scrolls, and the Ark of the Covenant. They alone were charged with conducting ceremonies and worship services.

One day, a woman rushed into the courts of the tabernacle. In her distress, she pleaded for the priest to intercede on her behalf. Her name was Hannah. In all the years of her marriage, she had not borne children to her husband Elkana. Elkana was so concerned about this—because he was from a proud line of Levites who settled in Ephraim—that he took another wife, Peninna, and she bore him sons and daughters. She constantly ridiculed Hannah, signifying that the Lord had no use for her. Hannah was so hurt that she would not even eat when the family went to Shiloh for the Feast (1 Samuel 1:4–8 cf.; Deuteronomy 16:13–15). She arose after the Feast days, went to the sanctuary and cried out to God for a son.

Eli the priest thought she was drunk, but Hannah refused to be turned away. She explained to Eli that she was pouring out her heart to God. This was her way of making an "unspoken prayer request," hoping that Eli would intercede. He blessed her and she went her way. She was so relieved that she sat down and ate—smiling.

The next day, Elkana and the family left Shiloh to go home. This was the last time Eli would see Hannah for three or four years but she was going to have a baby, and she knew it.

Samuel's Birth

She gave birth to a healthy baby boy and named him Samuel, meaning "heard of God" or "asked of God." The son stayed home with Hannah until he no longer needed her nursing. Then she went to Shiloh to dedicate him. In her prayers for a son, she had promised God that if He gave her a son she would commit Him to the Lord's service all the days of his life.

At Shiloh, Hannah kept her vow. She told Eli that Samuel was staying with him. How could Eli refuse? Especially after the miraculous work that God had done for Hannah!

Overcome with the joy of the Lord, Hannah burst into prayer, praising God in a sing–song fashion. The prayer was so captivating and memorable that Jesus' mother borrowed from it over 1000 years later, when she had a similar experience (cf. Luke 1:39–56).

Samuel's Preparation

Samuel's upbringing in the temple of Shiloh was excellent. Imagine him learning to read with the actual scrolls upon which were written the Law of Moses, having more access to the Holy Writ than even the priests who visited from other cities. He was an eyewitness to the sacred ceremonies and rites, and he administered them in some capacity; even ceremonies that were attended by Israelites from all over the world.[1] His mentor, the high priest himself, Eli, became like a father to him.

In those days, Israel was a nation ruled by God, a theocracy; the Law of Moses was its constitution, and the priests and

Levites were its executive body. Several times, the people of Israel fell into sin, and God allowed them to be oppressed by other nations. That Israel had fallen into sin was evident even on the level of priesthood. Hophni and Phinehas, the sons of Eli indulged in some of the most scandalous activities ever reported of priests.[2]

The two sons had absolutely no regard for the Lord (1 Samuel 2:12–17, 22–25). They interrupted sacrifices to take the meat that people offered on the altar. Even though he and his brother had sex with the women who worshiped at the door of the Tabernacle of the Congregation, Phinehas was a married man (4:19). Eli knew about his sons' wickedness, (2:22, ff.) but did not punish them.

But "the child Samuel grew in stature, and in favor both with the Lord and men" (2:26, NKJV, cf. Luke 2:52).

Samuel's Call

One night, when he was 12 years old God called Samuel three times. Each time, Samuel ran into Eli's room, thinking the voice was Eli's, and each time Eli told him that it was not. The third time, Eli realized the voice must have been from God and instructed the young man to respond to the next call by saying, "Speak, Lord, for your servant hears" (1 Samuel 3:8, NKJV). Samuel did so, and God used him as a mouth piece. His word spread throughout Israel. The people knew that God had raised a new prophet.

The Israelites waged war against the Philistines.[3] The Israelites were defeated in the first battle. The elders knew that the loss was due to more than physical power. Both they and the Philistines entered into warfare with the idea that God or gods were strategizing in favor of their respective armies to guide the war's fate. So, in their arrogance, the Israelite elders sent men to Shiloh to bring the Ark of the Covenant to the front lines. This was meant to manipulate the Lord, and who else but Hophni and Phinehas showed up at the battlefield bearing the Ark? (4:2–4)

The Philistines won a great victory that day, slaughtering over 30,000 soldiers, killing Hophni and Phinehas, and snatching the Ark. What a miserable day in Israel. The nation's most prized possession, the Ark was gone.

Eli heard of his sons' death, but when he was told about the Ark, the old man fell off his chair, broke his neck and died.

The Ark did not stay long in the hands of the Philistines. God devastated the city where the temple stood with tumors (emerods) and death.[4] After sending the Ark to three cities, the Philistines finally returned it to Israel.

Samuel's Message

Over the next 20 years, Israel began to turn back to God, no doubt as a result of holy agitation by Samuel. Even so, the Israelites held on to foreign deities, practicing the fertility rites that were typical of the surrounding nations. But Samuel addressed the Israelites, still under the jurisdiction of the Philistines, with a spiritual ultimatum: "If you return to the Lord, with all your heart, then put away the foreign gods and Ashtoreths from among you, and prepare your hearts for the Lord, and serve Him only: and He will deliver you from the hand of the Philistines" (7:5, NKJV).

As the Israelites began to put away their idols, Samuel called a meeting at Mizpah, a town in Benjamin, twelve and a half miles south of Shiloh. His influence and popularity by that time had to have been tremendous because he wanted all Israel to come to this meeting. At Mizpah he held a convocation (7:5–13a). The effect unified Israel as a God–fearing nation once again.

Samuel's message was not a simple speech or sermon, it included several audio–visual devices and physically involved the audience. The event at Mizpah is beautifully outlined into seven points, making it an excellent reference for a week–long revival:

1. The Israelites drew water and poured it out unto the Lord.

2. They fasted.

3. They confessed.

4. Samuel judged the congregation.

5. The Philistines gathered to attack the Israelites.

6. Samuel sacrificed a burnt offering.

7. Everyone praised God.

After the sacrifice was made, the men of Israel, though un-trained in warfare, were victorious over the Philistines. But no one took the glory for the victory. They all realized that it was the result of God's wonder–working power. Samuel erected a monument to the glory of God for His deliverance, and it was several years before the Philistines harassed Israel again (7:13).

In order to maintain the high level of spirituality in Israel, Samuel became a circuit–riding minister.[5] The task of making decisions and training leadership in various parts of the country was awesome. He set up his headquarters in Ramah, his hometown. He went from there to Bethel to Gilgal to Mizpah and back to Ramah.

Samuel took with him young prophets and priests, training them as they traveled together. This is called a "peripatetic school." The apprentices learned firsthand the work of the minis-try and duplicated it in their own towns. Evidently, the school continued after Samuel's death. Some commentators suppose it produced such leaders as Elijah and Elisha. Possible appearances of this "school of prophets" in Scripture may be 1 Samuel 10:5–11; 19:18–20; 1 Kings 20:35; 2 Kings 2:3.

Samuel's Sons

As Samuel grew old, he appointed his sons Joel and Abijah to judge over Israel. But his two sons abused the office in a way reminiscent of Hophni and Phinehas. They took bribes and cor-rupted the justice system.

The elders all over the country met together and agreed that it was time to install a king. They presented their request to Samuel (1 Samuel 8:1–6).

This distressed Samuel, and he prayed. God told him that they were not just rejecting him, but the Lord was their leader. God told Samuel to warn them of what to expect of their new king. A king would: draft their sons into his standing army; make them serve in his plantations; exercise dominion over their possessions, livestock and real estate; and levy taxes. Their king would oppress them and they would cry out for relief, but God would not listen (8:6–18).

Samuel and Saul

Still, the elders demanded a king. They wanted to be like all the other nations.

So God gave them a king. Samuel anointed Saul the son of Kush, a Benjaminite. Saul was the handsomest man in all Israel and the people were elated. "Long live the king!" they shouted (10:24, NKJV).

Samuel still judged Israel, and Saul's reign was not without conflict. The contention culminated when Samuel told Saul to completely eradicate the Amalekites, their possessions, their livestock, and everything else. Saul attacked the Amalekites and defeated them but held the king captive and brought back some of the sheep and cattle to sacrifice to the Lord. Samuel told Saul, "To obey is better than sacrifice," and that God rejected him as king (15:22).

Samuel and David

Samuel anointed David the second king of the tribe of Judah. After David killed Goliath, his popularity began to rise as a military leader. Saul became jealous of David's fame and vowed to kill him (18:5–11). As a political refugee, David fled to Samuel.

Samuel died before David took his position on the throne. All of Israel mourned the death of Samuel who played such a pivotal role in their national history (25:1).

Samuel's Leadership Qualities

In analyzing the leadership of Samuel, one notices that, first of all, he was submissive. Not only was he submissive to God's will but also to Eli's, who trained him, and to his mother, who sent him away from home. Eli was Samuel's teacher, and Samuel respected him by virtue of his authority. Even when Samuel had to pronounce God's judgment on Eli, he seemed somewhat hesitant, not wanting to disrespect his instructor.

Samuel could have bucked against his mother for making him stay away from his family. He only saw his whole family once a year (2:19). His submission to God's will instilled in him a generally yielding attitude to those who deserved his respect.

Samuel stayed pure. As he grew, he "was in favor both with the Lord and also with men" (2:26). Eli's sons Phinehas and Hophni brought shame on the priesthood. But Samuel never compromised his morality, he remained in favor with God.

After undergoing rigorous preparation throughout his childhood, Samuel was equipped to assume his role as the national leader when his time came. In 1 Timothy 3:6, Paul declared that in order to be an elder, the candidate must not be a novice, meaning that he must have adequate skill and background to perform his expected duties.

Samuel was a skilled administrator. He organized a spiritual "rally" at Mizpah, involving the whole nation (1 Samuel 7:1–6). He set up a yearly itinerary to tour the country, preaching, teaching and conducting worship (7:16–17). He established a school of prophets to prepare young servants of the Lord for the ministry.

He was prayerful. The meeting at Mizpah was originally publicized as a mass prayer meeting (7:5). The Israelites recognized him as a "prayer warrior," and told him never to stop crying to the Lord on their behalf (7:8a). With all the organizational skills and education that leaders have, prayer is necessary for God's blessing on their ministry. Samuel was an intercessor.

He prayed for the flock over whom the Lord placed him. Prayer is a powerful instrument of leadership.

Finally, Samuel was a parent for Israel. He was a strong, wise, and approachable authority figure. When Saul became jealous and turned against David, the first place David fled was to Samuel's house (19:18). He found comfort, trust and refuge in Samuel. Saul, too, had a high level of confidence in Samuel. Saul was so attached to Samuel as a source of wisdom and direction that he tried to consult him after he died! (28:3–25)

SCRIPTURE FOCUS

1 SAMUEL 1:9 So Hannah rose up after they had eaten in Shiloh, and after they had drunk. Now Eli the priest sat upon a seat by a post of the temple of the Lord.

10 And she was in bitterness of soul, and prayed unto the Lord, and wept sore.

11 And she vowed a vow, and said, O Lord of hosts, if thou wilt indeed look on the affliction of thine handmaid, and remember me, and not forget thine handmaid, but wilt give into thine handmaid a man child, then I will give him unto the Lord all the days of his life, and there shall no razor come upon his head.

20 Wherefore it came to pass, when the time was come about after Hannah had conceived, that she bare a son, and called his name Samuel, saying, Because I have asked him of the Lord.

24 And when she had weaned him, she took him up with her, with three bullocks, and one ephah of flour, and a bottle of wine, and brought him unto the house of the Lord in Shiloh: and the child was young.

25 And they slew a bullock, and brought the child to Eli.

26 And she said, Oh my lord, as thy soul liveth, my lord, I am the woman that stood by thee here, praying unto the Lord.

27 For this child I prayed; and the Lord hath given me my petition which I asked of him:

28 Therefore also I have lent him to the Lord; as long as he liveth he shall be lent to the Lord. And he worshipped the Lord there.

1 SAMUEL 3:1 And the child Samuel ministered unto the Lord before Eli. And the word of the Lord was precious in those days; there was no open vision.

2 And it came to pass at that time, when Eli was laid down in his place, and his eyes began to wax dim, that he could not see;

3 And ere the lamp of God went out in the temple of the Lord, where the ark of God was, and Samuel was laid down to sleep;

4 That the Lord called Samuel: and he answered, Here am I.

5 And he ran unto Eli, and said, Here am I; for thou calledst me. And he said, I called not; lie down again. And he went and lay down.

6 And the Lord called yet again, Samuel. And Samuel arose and went to Eli, and said, Here am I; for thou didst call me. And he answered, I called not, my son; lie down again.

7 Now Samuel did not yet know the Lord, neither was the word of the Lord yet revealed unto him.

8 And the Lord called Samuel again the third time. And he arose and went to Eli, and said, Here am I; for thou didst call me. And Eli per-

ceived that the Lord had called the child.

9 Therefore Eli said unto Samuel, Go, lie down: and it shall be, if he call thee, that thou shalt say, Speak, Lord; for thy servant heareth. So Samuel went and lay down in his place.

10 And the Lord came, and stood, and called as at other times, Samuel, Samuel. Then Samuel answered, Speak; for thy servant heareth.

SCRIPTURE SEARCH

Match the columns.

1. Samuel	A. Nation ruled by God
2. Hannah	B. Samuel's mentor
3. Eli	C. Nation ruled by a king
4. Theocracy	D. Samuel's mother
5. Monarchy	E. Submissive, pure, administrator, prayerful parent for Israel

The African American Connection

1. Prayer Is Important

A first lesson we can learn from the life of Samuel is taught to us by his mother, Hannah. When she was barren and Peninnah made fun of her, she didn't retaliate but took the problem to the One who could do something about it. The problems in our communities that we can do something about, we should handle. The problems that are beyond our control, we should not hesitate to "take to the Lord in prayer." Positive social change is the result of a working partnership between ourselves and the Lord. When we pray, we acknowledge and call upon our Senior Partner who specializes in making possible the impossible.

2. Skill and Character Are Important

We can glean a second lesson from the fact that Samuel was well trained and of moral character when he took office. He is a model for African American leadership. Should young people be placed into positions in the church when they have not demonstrated adequate qualifications? Should a person be given an office simply because, "He or she sounds good when preaching," or, "He or she knows how to lead a church service," or because "The pastor is old and this is the next best minister?" Should leaders be installed just because they can stir a crowd?

Shouldn't leaders be qualified according to biblical guidelines of purity and gravity? (1 Timothy 3:1–13) And when leaders violate these precepts, should they not submit to proper discipline?

3. Roots Are Important

Samuel remembered from whence he came. Is there a third important lesson for some of us here? When Samuel began riding the circuit, his itinerary started and ended in Ramah, his hometown, where his parents and probably all of his brothers and sisters lived. Though he saw them infrequently during his childhood, he still felt strongly attached.

African American Christian leaders who attend predominantly white schools for their biblical training often become estranged from their native community. The beautiful, rich African American heritage should be respected by leaders and taught to people. This has a unifying effect on us and helps us to love and respect each other as persons and contributors to our mutual survival and success.

4. What Do You Think?

A. What are some examples of conflicts between African American culture and Christianity?

B. What are examples of conflicts between commitment to African American culture and commitment to Christianity?

C. When there is a conflict between our culture and our Christian commitment, to which should we give our highest allegiance? Why?

D. What are examples of harmony between African American culture and Christianity?

E. What are some principles from the life of Samuel that can be applied to life in African American communities today?

CHAPTER EIGHT

A BOY FROM THE 'HOOD

Let's Discover . . .

Can God use a boy to liberate his country? Build a city? And help a nation worship?
Let's discover how God can use a boy, a sling, a mind and a harp to win victories, establish a nation and cause generations to sing.

DAVID:
A Boy from the 'Hood

Chaplain Melody L.H. Goodwin
1 Samuel 16:11-13; 2 Samuel 7:1-3, 14-17

David was the second king of Israel and reigned from 1000–962 B.C.[1] He lived in Bethlehem with his family and was the youngest of nine children (1 Chronicles 2:13–16). As a boy, he looked after his father's sheep and was anointed king by Samuel. But it wasn't until David was 30 that he actually became king of Israel. He reigned for a total of 40 years, in Hebron over Judah seven and a half years and over Israel and Judah 33 years (2 Samuel 5:4–5). David obeyed God. God was with him and made him prosperous (1 Samuel 16:13; 1 Kings 2:1–4).

David had eight wives and 19 sons. The sisters of David's sons are mentioned but there is no clear listing of his daughters, except Tamar (1 Chronicles 3:9). David's life story is told in parts of the first and second Books of Samuel, and the first Books of Kings and Chronicles. In 1 Kings 1—2:12, we have a glimpse of David's last days as he relinquishes his throne and makes his son, Solomon, king of Israel. In 1 Chronicles 29:26–28, we learn that David died, having enjoyed a long life of wealth and honor.

David: Man of Many Roles
Throughout the Bible, we see David in the roles of shepherd, musician, warrior, fugitive, king, father, saint and prophet.

First, we see David as a shepherd boy caring for his father's sheep. He was the youngest son of Jesse and spent many days in the fields (1 Samuel 16:11). David tells of how a bear and a lion came on two occasions and tried to carry off one of the sheep. He rescued the sheep and when the lion and bear turned on him, he seized them by the hair and killed them (17:34–36).

Second, we see David being anointed as king by Samuel. This was done after Saul was rejected by God as king of Israel. But David did not officially become king of Israel until Saul's death (1 Samuel 31; 2 Samuel 2).

Third, we see David as musician. God became angry with Saul and allowed an evil spirit to torment him. Saul's attendants suggested that he allow someone to play music for him to soothe him when the evil spirit flared up in him. They suggested David. David was sent to him and played his harp so well that the evil spirit departed Saul for a while. David then became Saul's musician (1 Samuel 16:23). The Psalms are filled with many of David's beautiful songs.

Fourthly, David became a warrior. David's first battle was with Goliath, the Philistine giant. He defeated Goliath and cut off his head. Saul was so impressed with David, he requested that Jesse, David's father allow him to stay with Saul as his armor bearer. Saul sent David out on several military exposi-tions. David won every battle. Because of his successes, Saul gave him a high military position and finally promoted him to leader of the entire army (1 Samuel 18:5).

Fifth, David became a fugitive. One day after returning from a successful battle against the Philistines, the women came out singing: "Saul has slain his thousands, and David his ten thousands" (1 Samuel 18:7). This made Saul very angry and jealous of David. He feared that since David al-ready had the hearts of the people, next he would take Saul's kingdom. David was then demoted from leader of the entire army, to leader of 1,000 men. David did not argue or com-plain but served loyally.

God was with David and he continued to win every battle he fought. All Israel and Judah loved him, which made Saul more and more afraid of him (1 Samuel 18:6–16). Twenty–one times Saul tried to kill David. Therefore David resorted to seeking refuge with the Philistines. They were powerful enough to protect him against Saul and his army. For about two years, he was on the run. It was not until Saul died that David was able to come back to Judah without fearing for his life.[2]

David eventually became king in Hebron and then king of all Israel. But his role as king in Hebron was not an easy one. He had to flee for his life and fight many battles before he became king over Israel. Actually, ten to twelve years passed between the time that David was anointed until he officially became king (1 Samuel 16—2 Samuel 2).[3]

After Saul died, all the tribes of Israel came and asked David to be king over all Israel (2 Samuel 5:1–3). As king over Israel David still had many battles to fight. Some were military battles and others were battles with his own sons. On at least one occasion, David had to flee for his life for fear his own son would killed him. But God restored David to his throne and he lived to become Israel's most revered king.

Dr. Herbert Lockyer, in *All the Men of the Bible* has suggested that David was also a saint and a prophet.[4] Both Christians and Jews accept David as a special child of God and acknowledge that the general trend of his life was spiritual (1 Samuel 13:14; 1 Kings 15:5).[5] David is known as "a man after God's own heart."

When David violated a divine law (Deuteronomy 17:17; 2 Samuel 5:13) and was rebuked by Nathan the prophet (for having Uriah killed), David's character was stained. His confession was heartfelt and sincere, though. He humbled himself before God. His confession as seen in Psalms 21 and 51, was a deep cry for pardon and restoration. When we sin, our confession should not be a cold, formal acknowledgement of guilt. It should be as David's: "Have mercy on me, O God, according to your unfailing love; according to your great compassion blot out my transgression" (Psalm 51:1, NIV).

When we sin, we should acknowledge the wrongful deed, ask for forgiveness and accept God's pardon and assurance with gratitude (1 John 1:9).

Finally, David had a prophetic gift. The spirit of God dwelt with David. Before every battle, David consulted God. God would tell David whether or not he would win that particular battle. This would determine whether or not David would fight. He chose not to fight battles that God told him he would not win. The Holy Spirit moved on David to set forth many truths that are related to the coming of Christ, the Messiah. In the New Testament, the Psalms are quoted more than any other part of the Old Testament.

David: Man of Achievement

David made three major accomplishments: (1) he conquered Israel's enemies; (2) he returned the Ark of the Covenant to Jerusalem; and (3) he planned and gathered the material for the building of the temple.

David conquered all of Israel's enemies, including the Philistine giant, Goliath. While a fugitive, David went to live with the Philistines and convinced them that he was against King Saul and Israel. Then David and his band of social rejects killed the entire populations of several towns. When asked by the king of Philistia about his bloody behavior, he lied and said that he had destroyed one of the towns in Israel. The king believed him.

After the Philistines killed Saul's son, Jonathan, Saul committed suicide. David became king and defeated all of Israel's enemies (1 Samuel 7:1 and 2 Samuel 8).

David's second major achievement was returning the Ark of the Covenant to Jerusalem. David took 30,000 chosen men to Baalah of Judah and retrieved the Ark. They danced before the Lord with songs, harps, lyres, tambourines, sistrums and cymbals. As the Ark was entering Jerusalem, David danced before the Lord, sacrificed burnt and fellowship offerings, and constructed a tent to house the Ark (2 Samuel 6 and 1 Chronicles 15).

David's third major accomplishment was the planning and gathering of material for building the temple in Jerusalem. He was not allowed by God to build it because he was a warrior and had shed the blood of many people (1 Chronicles 28:3). But God did allow him to prepare everything that was needed for the temple.

At the time, David's son Solomon was probably too young and inexperienced to know what was needed to construct the temple, but God had chosen him to be the builder. So David gave Solomon the plans for the temple, and he designated the weight of the gold, silver, bronze, iron, wood, onyx, turquoise, stones, gems and marble for each object used in the temple. He provided instructions for the organization of the priests and Levites and the articles to be used in the service of the Lord.

To show his commitment to the building of the temple, David donated to the "Temple Building Fund" 110 tons of gold and 260 tons of refined silver. After all these preparations, David called all the people together and gave encouraging words and specific orders to all the leaders of Israel to help Solomon complete the project.

Perhaps David's greatest contribution to the people of Israel and the world was his example of a life committed to worshiping God and serving His people.

Much of David's behavior was below standards later set by Jesus Christ (Matthew 5:27–28, 43–44), but as a result of David's refusal to worship any god but Jehovah, Israel enjoyed a time of peace and prosperity. During David's and most of Solomon's reign, the Jews enjoyed their Golden Age and David is revered as a model leader, a man who did right in the sight of the Lord (2 Chronicles 34:2).

David: An Effective Leader

In Dr. Bennie Goodwin's book, *The Effective Leader,* he makes five assumptions about effective leaders.[6] They are:

1. Every normal person can lead some group, somewhere, at some time.
2. Potential leaders are born, effective leaders are made.
3. Effective leaders are the result of opportunity, training and experience.
4. The only way to learn to lead is to lead.
5. Every normal Christian is expected to lead in the area of his or her gifts, talents and skills.

Assumptions two, three and four are ways of looking at David as an effective leader.

David is a prime example of the second assumption, that potential leaders are born but effective leaders are made. David was open to being made a leader. He was born into a line of great leaders—Abraham, Moses and Joshua. But that did not automatically make him a leader.

When David went to live in Saul's court, he was given several responsibilities. First he was put over a small unit of the army. This provided David an opportunity to watch and learn from more experienced military leaders. He was so successful with the small group that Saul eventually put him in charge of his entire army. Dr. Goodwin states that success in leadership has not so much to do with an inherited quality as with the climate in which a quality or qualities are allowed to be expressed and developed.

Dr. Goodwin's third assumption is that effective leaders are the result of opportunity, training and experience. Another of David's leadership qualities was his ability to take negative situations and turn them into growth opportunities. David seized a grand opportunity when he went to take food to his brothers, who were in battle with Goliath. David used the time for bringing food to his brothers to learn about the military and talk with the soldiers. Instead of only being a delivery boy, he decided to turn his visit into a military classroom.

Training and experience were soon to follow. Saul sent David out to fight many battles. "Whatever Saul sent David to do, he did it so successfully that Saul gave him rank in his army" (1 Samuel 18:5).

Dr. Goodwin's fourth assumption, the only way to learn to lead is to lead, highlights another of David's leadership qualities. David did not give up under pressure. His fugitive days are a clear summation of how effective leaders act when under pressure. Saul put out the word that he wanted David killed. David literally had to run for his life.

Instead of giving up or complaining about his situation, David continued to acquire more and more men and wealth. He led his men on crusade after crusade with continued success. Finally, after years of being under constant pressure and running for his life, David became the official king of Judah. Even though David was on the run, he learned to lead men and to seek God in every circumstance of his life.

David had a gift of love and inspired others to love. His concern for his people was very apparent. He was not a selfish man. When he went on his exploits, he returned with food, clothes, gold, silver and cattle for everyone to enjoy. Because of his unselfish nature and love for his people, they followed David into battle after battle and when he returned, they sang his praises.

David was a person who got the right things done by the right people at the right time and place. He knew how to motivate people. He was a learning, growing and productive leader who loved God and his people.

SCRIPTURE FOCUS

1 SAMUEL 16:11 And Samuel said unto Jesse, Are here all thy children? And he said, There remaineth yet the youngest, and, behold, he keepeth the sheep. And Samuel said unto Jesse, Send and fetch him: for we will not sit down till he come hither.

12 And he sent, and brought him in. Now he was ruddy, and withal of a beautiful countenance, and goodly to look to. And the Lord said, Arise, anoint him: for this is he.

13 Then Samuel took the horn of oil, and anointed him in the midst of his brethren: and the Spirit of the Lord came upon David from that day forward. So Samuel rose up, and went to Ramah.

2 SAMUEL 7:1 And it came to pass, when the king sat in his house, and the Lord had given him rest round about from all his enemies;

2 That the king said unto Nathan the prophet, See now, I dwell in an house of cedar, but the ark of God dwelleth within curtains.

3 And Nathan said to the king, Go, do all that is in thine heart; for the Lord is with thee.

14 I will be his father, and he shall be my son. If he commit iniquity, I will chasten him with the rod of men, and with the stripes of the children of men:

15 But my mercy shall not depart away from him, as I took it from Saul, whom I put away before thee.

16 And thine house and thy kingdom shall be established for ever before thee: thy throne shall be established for ever.

17 According to all these words, and according to all this vision, so did Nathan speak unto David.

SCRIPTURE SEARCH

Complete each word.
1. David and Jesus were born here: _ _T H L E _ _ _
2. David's original occupation: _ H _ P _ E _ D
3. David's hymn book:_ S _ L _ S
4. David's big project: the _ _ M P _ E
5. David's famous son: _ O L _ M _ _

The African American Connection

1. Talent and Skills

David was a multi–talented person. He was a singer, dancer, instrumentalist, poet, architect and administrator. a) Name two or three ways to encourage our people to discover and develop their talents and skills. b) Are there people who are naturally blessed with many talents? Or are these skills the results of opportunities and practice? c) What can the Black church do to create a climate where various ministries flourish?

2. Saints and Sinners

David was a true human being, a real person. He demonstrated that he was capable of rising high and falling low. He was a saint and a sinner. He was just like many leaders in the African American community, wasn't he? a) What did David do that might cause us to think of him as saintly? (See 1 Samuel 24:1–8; 2 Samuel 22:1–4.) b) What did David do that makes us know he was a sinner? (See 2 Samuel 11:1–27.) c) What are two or three things we can do to encourage our leaders to behave more saintly? (See 1 Timothy 4:12; 5:17–18.)

3. Love for Our People

David is perhaps most revered as a leader who was completely committed to the Lord and His people. a) Is it proper for African Americans to have a special love for each other, a love that does not include persons of other ethnic groups? (See Romans 1:16; 3:1–12; 9:1–5; 10:1.) b) Is it Christian to be "godly proud" to be an African American? (See Philippians 3:4–5, 7–11; Colossians 4:10–11.) c) Is it Christian to teach our children and youth to have a special appreciation for their African heritage? d) What are the advantages of teaching our children and youth about biblical people of African origin? e) Are there any disadvantages in teaching our children and youth about biblical people of African origin?

CHAPTER NINE

LORD, GIVE ME COMMON SENSE

LET'S DISCOVER . . .

===

Can God use a murderer's son to build a temple, to preserve wisdom, to extend an empire?
Let's discover how God can bring good out of bad, wisdom out of folly and life out of death.

===

SOLOMON:
Lord, Give Me Common Sense

Janifer Campbell
2 Chronicles 1:1, 6-12; 7:11-18

Solomon, also called Jedidiah, was the son of David and Bath-sheba. The story of his life is found in 1 Kings 1—11 and 2 Chronicles 1—9. The name Solomon or *Shlomo,* is derived from the Hebrew word *Shalom* meaning "peace." Its significance is revealed in the tranquil and prosperous years that characterized most of his life.

Born in Jerusalem, Solomon's life extended from 991 B. C. to 922 B. C. Solomon's birth illustrates God's absolute forgiving nature, as he was born to David and Bathsheba after the death of their first child who was conceived during their adulterous affair (2 Samuel 12:13–25). The biblical record reinforces God's loving grace; it states after the birth and naming of Solomon that "the Lord loved him." Because of the Lord's explicit affection toward Solomon, the Prophet Nathan was prompted to call him Jedidiah meaning, "Yahweh's beloved" (2 Samuel 12:24–25).

Solomon's African Heritage
Posterity remembers Solomon for his astonishing wisdom, ambitious construction projects, and fabulous wealth. While a study of Solomon "in all his glory" would prove to be very interesting, careful consideration must also be given to his ancestral roots. In the context of biblical history, perhaps one of the most significant contributions to African Americans in a study of Solomon is an awareness of the Black/African presence in Scrip-

ture. To be sure, after some 400 years of bondage on the continent of Africa, in the country of Egypt, intermingling between the indigenous population and the descendants of Abraham must have occurred.

Several prominent African personalities in the Bible have been identified by the diligent research of such African American scholars as Charles Copher, Cain Hope Felder, and Walter Arthur McCray.[1] A prime example of these biblical scholars' intense analysis is the work done to trace Solomon's African ancestry. McCray states the following regarding Solomon's mother Bathsheba:

> "The story of Bathsheba is recorded in 2 Samuel 11. Most know the story of David and Bathsheba. What is often overlooked is the fact that Bathsheba was married to Uriah the Hittite. It is widely known and accepted that the Hittites were a Hamitic people. They descended from Heth, a son of Canaan (Genesis 10:15; 23:10). If in fact Bathsheba shared the same ethnic origin as her husband (a not improbable assumption), then the child born to her and David, Solomon by name, did indeed have Black ancestry."[2]

A word study of Bathsheba's name would further support McCray's research that she was of African descent. Bathsheba is a combination of the Hebrew word *bath* meaning "daughter" and Sheba or *Sheh–bah,* an African nation which is translated "daughter of Sheba."[3]

What humble "pride" should beat in the hearts of African Americans with the knowledge that Bathsheba, Solomon and other prominent biblical characters share their ancestral heritage. Studying Scripture from this perspective provides information about numerous nations, tribes, people, and tongues and should further enhance African Americans' appreciation for God's inclusive plan of redemption.

Solomon's Ascension to the Throne

Solomon was a man of great astuteness. Under his leadership, the empire created by his father, King David, attained its highest potential. Solomon's ascension to the throne of Israel in 971 B. C. appears to have come about more as a result of intense conflict than from a smooth, humane transition (1 Kings 1—2).

David had many male offspring (1:9b), Solomon was not the eldest living son and by tradition, not the heir to Israel's throne. Since Solomon was not the eldest, it is difficult to determine what motivated him to want to be the successor to his father's throne as king of Israel. Was it a sense of duty or destiny, or a threat of loss of life?

The biblical narrative does not in any way suggest that he was a part of the counter–conspiracy initiated by Nathan, the prophet (1:11–14). Nor does it indicate that Solomon had an interest in the throne at any period prior to the counter–conspiracy. When deviation is made from tradition it is usually accompanied by conflict; and the explosive period preceding Solomon's brilliant career as ruler of Israel proved to be no exception.

When David was nearing the end of his life, Adonijah, his eldest living son, attempted to seize the throne by self–acclamation (1:5f). Reminded of his oath to Bathsheba, David officially named Solomon his successor, and he was anointed at Gihon by Zadok, the priest, and Nathan, the prophet. David's actions immediately caused Adonijah to realize that his plan to seize the throne was aborted. Sensing that his life was in danger, Adonijah sought refuge in the tabernacle by clinging to the horns of the altar (1:50).

The act was a symbolic way of requesting clemency. The altar represented the place where humankind received God's mercy. Solomon, no longer considering him a threat, granted Adonijah clemency on condition that he not make any further claims to the throne. Such acts of graciousness were characteristic of Solomon's reign. Adonijah's agreement to Solomon's conditions was shortlived. He soon conspired again to obtain the throne and, as a result, lost his life (2:13–25).

Solomon's Leadership Characteristics

As the newly appointed, youthful king of Israel, Solomon took his leadership responsibilities seriously. From a survey of his life, six positive leadership attributes can be identified. The first of these is humility.

During a sacrificial offering at Gideon, about five miles north of Jerusalem, the Lord revealed Himself to Solomon in a dream. The Lord invited him to ask for whatever he wanted. Recognizing the awesome responsibility leadership entails, the difficulty of making life and death decisions, coupled with the necessity of being a merciful and just ruler, Solomon requested a discerning heart tuned to the voice of the Lord so that he could lead the Israelites as the Lord would desire. The Lord was pleased by Solomon's humility and granted him a wise heart. In addition, God promised Solomon riches, honor and a long life if he would pursue the will of the Lord and obey His laws (3:11–14).

A second attribute of Solomon's leadership was his willingness to delegate authority. It is difficult for one person to be responsible for every facet of a group's well–being. This fact is greatly multiplied when an entire nation is to be considered. Solomon was wise enough not to attempt to run the nation's day–to–day affairs by himself and to see the necessity of sharing the responsibility of protecting, providing, and governing the Israelite Empire. He appointed 11 chief officials to oversee the affairs of state (4:1–6) and 12 district governors to supply provisions for the royal household (4:7–19).

Solomon did not place just anyone in positions of authority; rather, he chose people who were knowledgeable, experienced, and trustworthy.

A third attribute was Solomon's capacity for knowledge (4:29–34). Like Jesus who "increased in wisdom and stature, and in favor with God and man" (Luke 2:52), so did Solomon grow in knowledge and wisdom over an extended period. Even as all people came "to hear the wisdom of Solomon" (1 Kings 4:34),

111

he in turn, benefited from what they shared with him. He thereby corrected, improved, and sharpened his own knowledge base.

Solomon was a paragon of literary wisdom. The Scripture states that he "uttered three thousand proverbs and his songs were a thousand and five" (4:32). Evidence of his prolific writings have been preserved in the Book of Proverbs as well as in Ecclesiastes. One of his 1,005 songs is the "Song of Songs."[4] He also was an authority in botany and zoology (4:33).

Solomon was held in high esteem by his contemporaries. The Scripture states, "his wisdom surpassed the wisdom of all the people of the east, and all the wisdom of Egypt" (4:30), including Ethan the Ezrahite (whose name appears in the title of Psalm 89), Heman (a musician recorded in 1 Chronicles 15:19), Calcol, Darda, and other celebrated sages.[5]

Because of his capacity for knowledge, many important persons journeyed from faraway places to visit Solomon. He received them openly in his court. The purpose of these visits was not only to hear Solomon demonstrate his knowledge and wisdom, but also to test the authenticity of the rumors regarding his abilities. Such was the quest of the Queen of Sheba. Hearing of his fame, "she came to test him with hard questions" (1 Kings 10:1). This contest of wits resulted in Solomon satisfying her curiosity and surpassing her every expectation! Solomon so astonished her with his wisdom and prosperity that "there was no more spirit in her" (10:5).

The Queen of Sheba is a notable biblical figure of African descent. The Arabs called her Dikis and in Ethiopian legends she is referred to as Makeda.[6] Josephus, the ancient historian, records in his writings that she was the Queen of Egypt and Ethiopia.[7]

By way of her visit to King Solomon's court, this African queen attested to the affluence, abundance wealth and rich culture of her native land. The Queen of Sheba engaged Solomon with intellectual intrigue and lavished him with magnificent gifts (10:10). Indeed, this account dispels preposterous myths of Africa being a land void of cultural enlightenment and prosperity.

A fourth characteristic of Solomon's leadership was vision— for the people, the empire, and God. It was Solomon who said, "Where there is no vision, the people perish..." (Proverbs 29:18a). Apparently, Solomon took this need for vision very seriously.

All leaders are inheritors of pre–existing conditions over which they may have little or no control. Nevertheless, the mark of a leader is the ability to take a confusing situation and make it manageable for him/herself and intelligible for others. Solomon expressed his vision of justice in the maternal parenthood judgment (1 Kings 3:16–28), his vision of a functional government in his delegation of authority (4:1–19), his vision for a strong infrastructure and stable economy through conscription and trade (9:15–28), and his vision for the centrality of God in Israelite culture through the construction of the temple of Jerusalem (chapters 6—7).

Finally, for the Christian leader, whether pastor, chairperson or president, a close relationship with God is fundamental. In Solomon's construction of the temple, his relationship with God is more clearly evident than in other areas of his reign. This relationship is pivotal for every facet of Solomon's life and for every Christian leader. Solomon had a first–person relationship with God. For each leader this kind of relationship may exhibit itself in different ways, but a basic tenet of Christianity is that "you need to know God for yourself." With this relationship established, vision, the art of persuasion, and sustained action will multiply any leader's success.

Solomon's Final Years

God fulfilled His promise to Solomon to make him the wisest and wealthiest king on earth. During Solomon's reign, the nation of Israel reached magnificent heights of prosperity, international recognition and cultural achievement. In an effort to keep the nation in a peaceful and prosperous state, Solomon married many foreign wives which included the daughter of Pharaoh—another prominent person of African descent.[8] As a result, Solomon had a harem of 700 wives and 300 concubines.

A common practice in ancient times for rulers of differing kingdoms was to confirm a commercial or political treaty through a marriage. Contrary to Mosaic Law (Exodus 34:12–16; Deuteronomy 7:3–4), Solomon adhered to this common practice. He probably rationalized his actions as being harmless since he did not believe he had abandoned the Lord. As time elapsed, however, Solomon grew further away from God. He built shrines devoted to the worship of the gods of his foreign wives. This sacrilege angered God (1 Kings 11:9). It was for David's sake that God tempered His judgment with mercy and did not allow the kingdom to be divided during Solomon's lifetime. Nevertheless, the peace and tranquility that characterized his early rule vanished and was replaced with internal strife and external conflict (11:14–40). Solomon, whose life began as a manifestation of God's forgiving grace for a repentant heart, ended as a warning of God's judgment for those with divided allegiances.

SCRIPTURE FOCUS

2 CHRONICLES 1:1 And Solomon the son of David was strengthened in his kingdom, and the Lord his God was with him, and magnified him exceedingly.

6 And Solomon went up thither to the brasen altar before the Lord, which was at the tabernacle of the congregation, and offered a thousand burnt offerings upon it.

7 In that night did God appear unto Solomon, and said unto him, Ask what I shall give thee.

8 And Solomon said unto God, Thou hast shown great mercy unto David my father, and hast made me to reign in his stead.

9 Now, O Lord God, let thy promise unto David my father be established: for thou hast made me king over a people like the dust of the earth in multitude.

10 Give me now wisdom and knowledge, that I may go out and come in before this people: for who can judge this thy people, that is so great?

11 And God said to Solomon, Because this was in thine heart, and thou hast not asked riches, wealth, or honour, nor the life of thine enemies, neither yet hast asked long life; but hast asked wisdom and knowledge for thyself, that thou mayest judge my people, over whom I have made thee king:

12 Wisdom and knowledge is granted unto thee; and I will give thee riches, and wealth, and honour, such as none of the kings have had that have been before thee, neither shall there any after thee have the like.

2 CHRONICLES 7:11 Thus Solomon finished the house of the Lord, and the king's house: and all that came into Solomon's heart to make in the house of the Lord, and in his own house, he prosperously effected.

12 And the Lord appeared to Solomon by night, and said unto him, I have heard thy prayer, and have chosen this place to myself for a house of sacrifice.

13 If I shut up heaven that there be no rain, or if I command the locusts to devour the land, or if I send pestilence among my people;

14 If my people, which are called by my name, shall humble themselves, and pray, and seek my face, and turn from their wicked ways; then will I hear from heaven, and will forgive their sin, and will heal their land.

15 Now mine eyes shall be open, and mine ears attent unto the prayer that is made in this place.

16 For now have I chosen and sanctified this house, that my name may be there for ever: and mine eyes and mine heart shall be there perpetually.

17 And as for thee, if thou wilt walk before me, as David thy father walked, and do according to all that I have commanded thee, and shalt observe my statutes and my judgments;

18 Then will I stablish the throne of thy kingdom, according as I have covenanted with David thy father, saying, There shall not fail thee a man to be ruler in Israel.

SCRIPTURE SEARCH

Complete the sentences.

1. Solomon's mother was _____.
2. Solomon's request was for _____.
3. Solomon's famous African visitor was _____ _____ _____.
4. Solomon's great sin was building shrines to idol gods for some of his _____ wives.
5. Solomon's great architectural achievement was the building of the _____ in _____.

The African American Connection

1. God's Word: A Source of Insight

God's Word is not merely theoretical in nature. It speaks with relevant application to the human condition. The social problems that plague the African American community, such as drug abuse, teen pregnancy, inadequate levels of education, unemployment and underemployment, are opportunities for

116

Christian leaders to apply God's Word to uplift humanity.

In speaking to the African American experience, God's Word does not give simplistic solutions to the complex issues that confront its leaders. It does, however, furnish a process by which African American leaders, through prayerful analysis, can interpret their own unique circumstances and develop plans of appropriate action. Solomon's keen insight into human nature is an illustration of such a process.

Insight into basic human nature goes beyond making decisions based solely on external facts about persons and circumstances. It entails applying the holistic approach to viewing situations and circumstances from the perspective of all parties involved. It is crucial for every leader to understand how a problem is perceived, because the interpretation will have a direct bearing on the approach undertaken to solve it.

2. The Victims: Are They at Fault?

The method of dealing with life's problematic issues based exclusively on external facts is a process which William Ryan identifies as "blaming the victim."[9] Such a process interprets the external facts of inequality as being the victim's fault.

For example, when considering only external facts, solutions to the issue of poor education result only in treating the child rather than challenging an inferior institutional system of education.

3. Marva Collins: Educational Role Model

A wholistic approach to the challenge of poor educational achievement would recognize that the quality of education offered is the key to successful learning. A case in point is Chicago's Westside Preparatory School.

Disenchantment with the public school system, coupled with a concern for Black students who went from grade to grade not knowing how to read or write, prompted Marva

117

Collins to found a school in her home. "Most of the students who came to her [in 1975] have been labeled problem children," wrote Marilyn Marshall, author of an 1985 *Ebony* magazine article, "Marva Collins: Weathering the Storm:" "She has been determined to do what society often says can't be done: make achievers out of Black students who have been written off by the school system as failures."[10]

Marva Collins did not blame the victims for their victimization. Rather, she addressed the unproductive nature of their learning environment and challenged them to make the choice regarding their education. Marva Collins wrote a creed and requires her students to recite it daily: "I will ignore the tags and names given me by society since only I know what I have the ability to become. I will continue to let society predict, but only I can determine what I will, can or cannot do…"[11]

Her approach to learning resulted in empowering her students.

4. What Do You Think?

A. What are some of the elements of Marva Collins' approach that make it successful?

B. Can her school be used as a model for public school education in the African American community? Why or why not?

C. Can we use her school as a model for Christian education in the African American church? Why or why not?

D. Can Solomon's wisdom be attributed at all to his education?

E. Are there any similarities between Marva Collins and Solomon? If so, what are they?

CHAPTER TEN

STRANGE BUT POWERFUL

LET'S DISCOVER . . .

Can God use a strange person whose dress and behavior are odd? Whose words are tough and tender? Through whom God sends drought and fire, and restores the dead to life?

Let's discover how God uses a person who is different to remind us that all of our modern idols are deaf, dumb and blind; and that the God who responds to our prayers is the God who is real.

ELIJAH:
Strange But Powerful

Dr. Kenneth Hammonds
1 Kings 17:1-6; 18:30-39; 2 Kings 2:11

Elijah literally means "My God is Yahweh." This man's name clearly indicates his mission: to speak boldly for the only true God, Israel's God, Yahweh. Elijah is the greatest of the "Oral Prophets" (those not having a book named after them), but we know very little about his early life. We do know that he was from the town of Tishbe in Gilead, located on the eastern side of the Jordan River (1 Kings 17:1).

The area where he was born consists of large rolling plains and rocky hills, and the inhabitants were for the most part in solitude unless visited by a traveler or roaming bands of people. The people of the area were somewhat molded by the rocky nature of their surroundings; the area was used as shelter for exiles and was the site of military battles (2 Samuel 17:24–29). This environment produced a man who could act alone and preferred to do so, who seemed to be able to act without fear of any person. Of course, the interesting exception to that was a woman named Jezebel.

Elijah: Last Place in the Fashion Contest
Elijah would win no prize in Israel's "Annual Fashion Show." He is described as, "A hairy man wearing a leather belt around his waist" (2 Kings 1:8). The servants did not say that Elijah was a man with a hairy garment. The garment wrapped around his body was made of sheep, goat skin or possibly even coarse

camel hair. This manner of dress "was worn by the prophets, not as mere ascetics, but as preachers of repentance, the rough garment denoting the severity of divine judgments upon the effeminate nation, which reveled in luxuriance and worldly lust."[1] Elijah's dress was a message against the materialism and luxury of the kings and royalty he confronted.

Elijah's Life: A Dramatic Series

Elijah appears upon the scene shortly after the beginning of the reign of King Ahab of Israel (874–853 B.C.) and he is taken up into heaven probably at the beginning of the reign of King Joram (Jehoram) (852–841 B.C.). So Elijah's time of ministry was approximately 872–852 B. C., about 20 years.

The life of Elijah is full of drama and intrigue. The hero Elijah is in a continuing battle with the sinister Ahab and the evil forces of the idol god Baal. The prophet's life is recorded in the Books of 1 Kings 17 to 2 Kings 2.

Act 1: The Grand Entrance

"And Here He is…, Elijah the Tishbite!" Story Line (1 Kings 17:1–7) Ahab has begun his rule, and everything seems to be going fine. He follows in the evil footsteps of his father King Omri. He enjoys the worship of "other gods" and even marries a Baal worshiper, builds a temple and erects an altar to Baal in Samaria. For the most part, Israel is at peace with its sister nation Judah. The Northern Kingdom is prosperous and King Ahab looks forward to a bright future with his new wife, his new religion, and his new political career.

Everything seemed to be going fine, but Ahab has angered the LORD. Suddenly, like a bolt of lightning and a sudden clap of thunder on a quiet summer day, a man emerges dressed in animal skin, rough in appearance, and bold in his stance—Elijah the Tishbite bursts upon the scene. A single verse, 1 Kings 17:1, describes this grand entrance:

"And Elijah the Tishbite, of the inhabitants of Gilead, said to Ahab, 'As the Lord God of Israel lives, before whom I stand, there shall not be dew nor rain these three years, except at my word.'"

Immediately after this devastating prophecy, Elijah is instructed by the Lord to go east to the Brook Cherith which is near Tishbe. This prophecy is not only devastating to the people of that region, but it is also a "slap in the face" of Baal, considered the fertility god and god of vegetation and rain. Elijah takes a God–given break from his prophetic duties. God takes care of him and commands the ravens to bring food to him.

Act 2: (Scene 1) Elijah and the Widow

"Little People Are Important Too" Story Line (1 Kings 17:8–16)
After Cherith Brook dries up because of a drought, Elijah is told by the Lord to go to a widow in Zarephath, a nonbeliever in Yahweh. Zarephath is a town of Phoenicia, an area inhabited by African peoples. The widow has only enough food for herself and her son, but at the word of Elijah she believes the man of God and makes a small cake for Elijah first. The faith of this "unbeliever" is truly amazing! God rewards the Phoenician widow's faithfulness by keeping her jars of flour (KJV, "barrel of meal") and oil barrel full during the devastating drought.

Act 2: (Scene 2) The Miracle of Life

"A Son Is Raised from the Dead" Story Line (1 Kings 17:17–24)
Elijah is now very much welcomed in the widow's home. However, one day a tragedy strikes and the widow's son becomes seriously sick and dies. The widow wonders if opening her door to this stranger has caused her son's death. This son was so important to her, she wonders, "How could God do this to me?" Elijah carries the son to the upper room of the house. There he prays to Yahweh and stretches himself three times across the child, giving warmth to the boy. This is the first instance in Scripture of anyone being brought back to life.

Act 3: (Scene 1) Elijah and Ahab

"The Trouble Maker Returns" Story Line (1 Kings 18:1–19) It has been three years since Elijah prophesied about the lack of rain in the land. Because there is no rain there is a severe famine. Obadiah, one of the officials in Ahab's court, is with Ahab searching for green pasture areas for their livestock.

Suddenly (as usual), Elijah appears and asks Obadiah to get King Ahab. He wants to speak with him. However, just before Obadiah gets Ahab, he gives us some insight into the rapid appearances and far travels of Elijah. In verse 12 he tells Elijah that he is afraid to get Ahab because "as soon as I am gone from you, the spirit of the Lord will carry you to a place I do not know." Evidently, it is common knowledge for the people of Elijah's time to know about the "swift travel" of Elijah. Even the community of the prophets' sons in 2 Kings 2:16 speaks of searching for Elijah after his translation and they state, "perhaps the Spirit of the Lord has taken him up and cast him upon some mountain or into some valley."

Ahab and Elijah finally meet again after three years. Jezebel seems to be in charge. Ahab bellows in verse 17, "Is that you, O troubler of Israel?" Ahab usually lacks any true spiritual discernment and blames Elijah for Israel's problems caused by the drought. The Hebrew word for trouble means, to disturb, to afflict, to grieve. Ahab accuses Elijah of being a "trouble maker" and of "disturbing the peace." All was going well and according to plan for Ahab until Elijah suddenly showed up three years ago. Elijah, of course, being no milk toast immediately speaks boldly: "I have not troubled Israel, but you and your father's house have, in that you have forsaken the commandments of the Lord and have followed the Baals" (v. 18). Elijah tells Ahab to gather the prophets of Baal and Asherah, the female companion of Baal, and the people of Israel and meet him on Mount Carmel. For some unknown reason the prophets of Asherah did not show up.

Act 3: (Scene 2) The Great Challenge

"Would the Real God Please Show Up?" Story Line (1 Kings 18:20–40) It is time for a showdown. Elijah stands at what will be the greatest moment in the history of Israel since the miracles of Moses and Joshua. In verse 21 Elijah issues the challenge to the people of Israel: "How long will you falter between two opinions? If the Lord is God [the God], follow Him; but if Baal [is the God], follow him."

There is an interesting play on words in the Hebrew language here. The word translated "father" ("halt," KJV), is the same word translated "leaped" in verse 26 as "danced." Elijah is asking the people, "How long will you continue to jump around back and forth between opinions about who is THE TRUE God?" The NIV translates this phrase, "How long will you waver between two opinions?" The Jewish scholars of *The Jerusalem Bible* give the interesting translation, "How long will you go limping between two opinions?"

The people did not attempt to answer. They were condemned by their silence. They wished to combine the worship of Yahweh and Baal. Baal worship had many features of emotionalism, fanaticism and sensuality. Who would want to put down a religion that appealed so much to the desires of the flesh? However, in the very first commandment of the Decalogue, Yahweh has made it clear that there are to be no other gods besides Him.

The challenge is set forth. Two sacrifices will be set up and the God who answers by fire will be the true God. After all, Baal is a god of lightning and thunder; the answer by fire should be no difficulty for him. The prophets of Baal cry out for hours in verse 26, but "there are no voices; no one answered." Then they danced around and jumped on the altar, but still there was no answer.

Elijah repairs the broken down altar of Yahweh and offers a sacrifice. Three times he pours large pitchers of water over the sacrifice and around the altar. Elijah offers a simple prayer in contrast to the long prayers, frenzied emotionalism, and far out

124

fanaticism of the Baal religion. In verse 38 the fire of Yahweh falls upon the sacrifice and licks up the water that was in the surrounding trench. The people are so amazed with this spectacular display of power that they declare in verse 39, "The LORD, He is God! The LORD, He is God!" Yahweh, HE [is] THE God, Yahweh, HE [is] THE God.

Elijah puts the 450 prophets of Baal to death at Kishon Brook. Where are the 400 prophets of Asherah? Maybe they felt that this was a "male god thing" and that female gods should stay out of it! It turns out to their advantage that they aren't there. Then the drought finally ends, showing that the God of Israel is really the only true God of the earth.

Act 3: (Scene 3) Enter Jezebel

"Run for Your Life, Elijah!" Story Line (1 Kings 19:1–7) Elijah has had a great spiritual victory on Mount Carmel. But now Jezebel, the real power behind the throne and the real promoter of Baalism, has heard of the death of the prophets of Baal. She sends a messenger to tell Elijah in no uncertain terms that by tomorrow she will kill him like he killed the prophets of Baal. This great prophet, a rough and rugged mountain man, a man who communes with the Spirit, by whose word God stopped the rain for three years, who called the king to his face the trouble maker of Israel, who just called down fire from heaven in the greatest feat of this kind in history; yes, this great man is scared to death of Ahab's wife, the infamous Jezebel. Indeed, the man of God was so exhausted from spiritual battle that he believed the answer was found in running away from the conflict with evil.

Elijah traveled about 100 miles away to the South and prayed to God to die. What an interesting prayer. If he wanted to die he could have stayed in Israel and Jezebel would have gladly answered his prayer!

Time Out: Elijah, "Can We Talk?" (1 Kings 19:9–18)

Elijah now believes that he is the only true prophet of Yahweh left. First God feeds him, then Elijah goes to Mount Horeb, also called Mount Sinai—the place of the giving of the Ten Commandments—which takes him 40 days. There God reveals Himself to Elijah in a "still small voice."

Help Wanted: "Where Can I Find a Good Assistant?"

Elijah felt all alone, but God let him know that there are 7,000 in Israel, not counting Judah, who are true to Him. God decided to give Elijah some help, so He supplied several helpers, listed in the remaining chapters of 1 Kings, including God Himself:

1. Elisha (19:19–21), 2. a prophet (20:13), 3. a man of God (20:28), 4. A certain man of God (20:35, ff.), 5. sons of the prophets (20:35), and 6. Michaiah (22:1–28).

Act 4: The Grand Finale

"Wow, What an Ending!" Story Line (2 Kings 2:1–12) By this time Ahab has died in battle (1 Kings 22). Ahaziah, a son of Ahab, became king in 853 B.C. He was like his father in that he did not obey the voice of the Lord. After the death of Ahaziah another son of Ahab, Joram (Jehoram) began to rule in 852 B.C. This now brings us to the vivid exodus of Elijah from this world.

Elijah knows that the time of his departure is near, so he visits various communities of the prophets (also called sons of the prophets) at Bethel, Jericho, and a community near the Jordan River. Elisha requests that a double portion of the spirit of Elijah be upon him. Elijah says that if Elisha sees him being taken away, the request will be granted. Verse 11 describes this spectacular event: "Then it happened, as they continued on and talked, that suddenly a chariot of fire appeared with horses of fire, and separated the two of them, and Elijah went up by a whirlwind into heaven."

There should be no attempt to explain away this incident, but just an acceptance of the truth that Elijah left this earth as he lived in it: By the miraculous power of Yahweh the God of Israel. However, we must understand the spiritual nature of this event and see it in light of at least two important points: 1) a glimpse into the spirit realm and the power thereof, and 2) a preview of the future transformation of the believer in Christ.

So Elijah was in the midst of human struggle just like us. Through Elijah's show of courage, conviction, faithfulness, and prayer God teaches us that He will sustain us through the difficulties of any contemporary problem. Elijah was only a frail human being empowered to victory by the omnipotent God.

SCRIPTURE FOCUS

1 KINGS 17:1 And Elijah the Tishbite, who was of the inhabitants of Gilead, said unto Ahab, As the Lord God of Israel liveth, before whom I stand, there shall not be dew nor rain these years, but according to my word.

2 And the word of the Lord came unto him, saying,

3 Get thee hence, and turn thee eastward, and hide thyself by the brook Cherith, that is before Jordan.

4 And it shall be, that thou shalt drink of the brook; and I have commanded the ravens to feed thee there.

5 So he went and did according unto the word of the Lord: for he went and dwelt by the brook Cherith, that is before Jordan.

6 And the ravens brought him bread and flesh in the morning, and bread and flesh in the evening; and he drank of the brook.

1 KINGS 18:30 And Elijah said unto all the people, Come near unto me. And all the people came near unto him. And he repaired the altar of the Lord that was broken down.

31 And Elijah took twelve stones, according to the number of the tribes of the sons of Jacob, unto whom the word of the Lord came, saying, Israel shall be thy name:

32 And with the stones he built an altar in the name of the Lord: and he made a trench about the altar, as great as would contain two measures of seed.

33 And he put the wood in order, and cut the bullock in pieces, and laid him on the wood, and said, Fill four barrels with water, and pour it on the burnt sacrifice, and on the wood.

34 And he said, Do it the second time. And they did it the second time. And he said, Do it the third time. And they did it the third time.

35 And the water ran round about the altar; and he filled the trench also with water.

36 And it came to pass at the time of the offering of the evening sacrifice, that Elijah the prophet came near, and said, Lord God of Abraham, Isaac, and of Israel, let it be known this day that thou art God in Israel, and that I am thy servant, and that I have done all these things at thy word.

37 Hear me, O Lord, hear me, that this people may know that thou art the Lord God, and that thou hast turned their heart back again.

38 Then the fire of the Lord fell, and consumed the burnt sacrifice, and the wood, and the stones, and the dust, and licked up the water that was in the trench.

39 And when all the people saw it, they fell on their faces: and they said, The Lord, he is the God; the Lord, he is the God.

2 KINGS 2:11 And it came to pass, as they still went on, and talked, that, behold, there appeared a chariot of fire, and horses of fire, and parted them both asunder; and Elijah went up by a whirlwind into heaven.

SCRIPTURE SEARCH

Complete the sentences.
1. The name _____ means "my God is _____."
2. Elijah was born in _____.
3. Elijah prophesied during the time when _____ was king.
4. A decisive confrontation between Yahweh and Baal took place on Mt. _____.
5. It was there that God answered by _____.

The African American Connection

1. Is God Interested?
What incidents in Elijah's life remind African Americans that God is interested in them?

2. Need a Break?
What can today's servants of God learn form Elijah's need to take a break? Is leader "burnout" a chief source of "dropout" today for many Christians? How frequently should our leaders take breaks to refresh themselves in the midst of a spiritual

battle? What can a leader expect from God during such times of refreshment? What part do congregations play in giving pastors "a break?"

3. Who's on the Fence?

Are many of our people "straddling the fence?" Is it possible to worship the God of the Bible on Sunday and "do our own thing" the rest of the week? What does Elijah's challenge, "If God be God then serve Him alone," mean to those who want to be part of an answer to a problem rather than part of the problem?

4. Am I Alone?

Is it possible to forget just how victorious we have been in spiritual battles against the forces of evil, and to retreat and feel sorry for ourselves? Are leaders especially prone to these feelings? What are some "helps" that we can use to keep us aware of the presence of God? What lessons can we learn from the interaction of Elijah with the widow and her son?

CHAPTER ELEVEN

IT'S NOT WHERE YOU COME FROM

LET'S DISCOVER . . .

*Can God use a teenager
to help people find their identity? To
stop the worship of false gods? To turn
people back to God's Word?
Let's discover how God uses young
people to challenge the status quo and
bring a new awareness of God's purposes,
power and peace!*

JOSIAH:
It's Not Where You Come From

Dr. Bennie Goodwin
2 Chronicles 34:1-3, 8, 15, 18-23, 27-28; 35:1, 17, 23-25

Josiah is a man with a single identity. He is known only as the king of Judah. He was selected king when he was only eight years old, served as king for 31 years and died with wounds he received in battle (2 Kings 22; 23:29–30). The primary sources of his life story are found in 2 Kings 21—23 and 2 Chronicles 33—36. The Prophet Jeremiah mentions him (Jeremiah 1:2; 22:11) and the Prophets Nahum, Habakkuk and Zephaniah were his contemporaries.

His father Amon was also a king, as were his grandfather, King Manasseh and his great–grandfather, King Hezekiah. Probably he was born in 647 B.C. in the palace in Jerusalem. He may have been born in Boscath, the home of his mother, Jedidah and grandmother, Adaiah, and brought to Jerusalem sometime later (2 Kings 22:1).

Although he died in 609 B.C., a relatively young man of 39 years old, Josiah is recognized as one of the truly outstanding leaders in the Bible. The writer of the Book of 2 Kings said, "He did that which was right in the sight of the Lord, and walked in all the way of David his father, and turned not aside to the right hand or to the left" (2 Kings 22:2).

This statement is especially remarkable because both his father, Amon and grandfather Manasseh were wicked kings (2 Kings 21:20). Josiah's life as a leader is important to us because it demonstrates what God can do through one person who is committed to being right and doing right. His life shows that in spite of growing up in a bad home, a bad neighborhood and a corrupt society, it is possible to live in contrast to our surroundings and by commitment to the Lord become an agent of positive spiritual and social change.

Josiah's Achievements

Josiah became king under very negative circumstances. His father King Amon had just been murdered by his own servants in his own house (2 Kings 21:19–26). Then other persons killed the servants who murdered Amon. On the heels of all this blood letting, eight–year–old Josiah was made king.

During the eight–year silence between 640 and 632 B.C., Josiah was probably being reared by his mother, under the influence of such persons as Hilkiah, the priest, Shaphan, the court secretary and perhaps Huldah, the prophetess. At the age of 16, he seems to have had an important personal, spiritual experience: "he began to seek after the God of David his father..." (2 Chronicles 34:3). It's interesting that he did not identify with either his father Amon or his grandfather Manasseh, both of whom were evil kings. In fact, he did not even identify with his great–grandfather, Hezekiah, who was a good king. No, he identified with his ancestor David, whom we know was not perfect in his behavior, but confessed and repented to show that his heart was right (Psalm 51). With King David, the greatest of all Jewish kings as his model, Josiah the teenager began a life of serious personal commitment to God.

A. He Rooted Out Idolatry. When Josiah turned 20 years old, he committed his life to social and spiritual change. He began a campaign against idolatry. Basically idolatry is the practice of worshiping false gods. What distinguished Jewish people from non–Jewish people was God's commitment to them and their commitment to their God Jehovah. This national covenant or agreement was initiated by God with Abraham, the father of the Jewish people, the person through whom all Jewish people trace their religious heritage.

133

Later when God gave the Ten Commandments to Moses, one of the first things He said was, "thou shall have no other gods before me...Thou shalt not make unto thee any graven image, or any likeness of any thing that is in heaven above, or that is in the earth beneath, or that is in the water under the earth. Thou shalt not bow down thyself to them, nor serve them" (Exodus 20:3–5a).

At 20 years old Josiah looked around and saw idolatry everywhere. Actually, idolatry was not a new experience for the Jews. All during their history they were "sometimes up and sometimes down and sometimes level with the ground" when it came to worshiping other gods. Idolatry seemed to be an ever–recurring problem for them. Remember the story of Aaron and the golden calf? (Exodus 32) Remember the problems during the time of the Judges? (Judges 2:11–19) Yes, idolatry was a continual problem. But it was during the time of the kings that idolatry reached its zenith and the Jews sank to their lowest point spiritually. Actually, it was Solomon who introduced idolatry on a grand scale and most of the kings of both Israel (the Northern Kingdom) and Judah (the Southern Kingdom) followed Solomon's example (1 Kings 11:1–11). With some success, Hezekiah, Josiah's great–grandfather tried to carry the Jews back to the worship of Jehovah. And then after a life of terrible indulgence in idolatry and indescribable violence, near the end of his life, his grandfather Manasseh tried to institute some reforms (2 Chronicles 33:11–17). Amon, Josiah's father didn't even try to extend Manasseh's reforms but instead plunged the nation back into idolatry. Although Amon was king only two years, "He did that which was evil in the sight of the Lord...and served the idols and worshipped them...and he forsook the Lord God of his fathers and walked not in the way of the Lord" (2 Kings 21:20–22).

We have given so much attention to idolatry because this was the primary religious–social problem of the Jewish people. And this is the first problem that Josiah attacked with all of his youthful strength and enthusiasm. He went out for the destruction of idolatry like Michael Jordan goes out for basketball, like Larry Holmes goes out for boxing, like Marva Collins goes out for education and like Michael Jackson goes out for dancing.

When you read the account in 2 Kings 23 and 2 Chronicles 34, you see words like purge, break down, burnt, cut down, break in pieces and made dust of. So the first thing Josiah did after making his personal commitment to God was to get rid of idolatry, the Jews' greatest curse.

B. He Repaired the Temple. By the time Josiah was 26 years old he had gotten rid of all the worship places dedicated to other gods. Next, he set about repairing the temple in Jerusalem. To do the extensive repairs and renovations on the 300–year–old temple required money. So Josiah raised the money, put it in the hands of the carpenters, builders and masons and the work on the temple proceeded (2 Kings 22:3–7).

C. He Restored the Law to Prominence. While the temple was being renovated, Hilkiah, the priest discovered a book that turned out to be a copy of the Law, most probably the Book of Deuteronomy. Hilkiah got excited and told Shaphan, the scribe, "I have found the book of the law in the house of the Lord" (2 Kings 22:8). Shaphan read the book and brought it to Josiah. When Josiah heard what was in the book and realized how far his people had strayed from what was in the book, he tore his robe in dismay and repentance. He then sent Hilkiah and Shaphan to ask Huldah, the priestess about the meaning of what they had discovered in the book.

Huldah had bad news and good news. She said that because of Judah's sins, particularly their idolatry, they were going to be punished severely. The nation was going to be captured and taken into slavery in Babylon. That was the bad news. The good news was that because of Josiah's tender heart and humble attitude, he was going to be spared God's judgment. Huldah said Josiah would die early so that he would not "see all of the evil" that God was going to permit the Jews to suffer (2 Kings 22:20).

135

After consulting with the Lord through Huldah, Josiah called all the people "both small and great" to the temple to hear the reading of the Book (23:2). After hearing the words of the Lord, the king and all of the people committed themselves "to walk after the Lord, and to keep his commandments...testimonies and his statues with all their heart and soul, and to perform the words of this covenant that were written in the book" (2 Kings 23:3).

D. He Revived the Celebration of the Passover. Josiah's fourth act of leadership was to reinstitute the celebration of Passover and to reinstate the full order of worship in the temple. It seems that whatever Josiah did, he did it wholeheartedly and so it was with the Passover. The event was celebrated in grand style. The priests and Levites, the singers and ushers were in place, and over 41,000 animals were sacrificed to the Lord. It was a celebration, the likes of which had not been experienced since "the days of Samuel, the prophet. Never did all the kings of Israel celebrate such a passover as Josiah and the priests, and the Levites, and all Judah and Israel were present, and the inhabitants of Jerusalem" (2 Chronicles 35:18).

E. He Restored Peace. The Passover celebration was Josiah's last recorded act of leadership. He died 13 years later in a battle with Egypt's Pharaoh–Necho. The pharaoh was on his way to join the Assyrians in their battle with the Babylonians. For some undisclosed reason, Josiah felt he should stop Necho. Necho tried to persuade Josiah against this course of action, but he was unsuccessful. It was in the battle at Megiddo that Josiah was mortally wounded and carried back to Jerusalem where he died. The Prophet Jeremiah wrote a special poem in his honor and the nation mourned his death (35:20–27).

Josiah had been an exceptionally good leader. "There had never been a king like him before, who served the Lord with all his heart, mind and strength, obeying all the law of Moses, nor has there been a king like him since" (2 Kings 23:25, TEV).

Josiah was actually the Jews' last "real" king. Less than 25 years after Josiah's death, the people of Judah were deported by King Nebuchadnezzar into Babylon where they stayed until the days of Nehemiah and Ezra.

Josiah's Leadership Qualities

The five major changes experienced by Judah were the result of Josiah's effective leadership. Josiah was an effective leader because he got the right things done through the right people at the right time and place.[1] How did he do it? What were some of his leadership characteristics that God used to bring about the needed changes?

We can identify five pairs of characteristics that account for Josiah's success as a religious leader. The first three pairs may be thought of as personal and spiritual. They are: (1) humility and obedience; (2) honesty and generosity and (3) reverence and compassion. The second pair of characteristics may be thought of as administrative and managerial: 4) decisive and thorough and 5) organized and committed.

Now let's examine each of these pairs and see how they were manifested in Josiah's life and how they helped make him an effective leader.

A. Humble and Obedient. Having been born into a long line of kings and become a king at the age of eight, it seems that Josiah would have been a natural victim of conceit and arrogance. Instead, when he was confronted with God's demands in the newly rediscovered Book of the Law, he actually tore his garment in contrition and wept.

The word of the Lord through the Prophetess Huldah said that Josiah's humility saved him from being part of Judah's ultimate downfall (2 Kings 22:19–20, LB). This humility of mind and spirit enabled him to listen, ask for help and be obedient. "He turned not aside to the right hand or to the left but obeyed the Lord completely" (2 Kings 22:2). He was able to get the right things done because he practiced doing right.

B. Honest and Generous. One of Josiah's great desires and accomplishments was the renovation of the temple. Josiah did not want his project sabatoged by accusations of misappropriated funds, so he did three important things: 1) he chose honest men to do the work; 2) he gave Hilkiah, the priest specific instructions about how the money was to be collected and spent; and 3) he required periodic reports from Shaphan, his executive secretary on how the work was progressing. He set the necessary procedures in place to demonstrate his honesty and to insure the same on the part of those who handled the money (2 Kings 22:3–7).

The Passover celebration of Josiah was unique in the history of the kingdom (2 Kings 23:22). The burnt offering alone consisted of over 41,000 animals. Josiah did not put the financial burden of the celebration on his people; instead, he generously donated 33,000 lambs, goats and bulls. His actions inspired other leaders who contributed an additional 8,400 animals (2 Chronicles 35:7–8).

C. Reverent and Compassionate. An effective leader appreciates the past and can envision the future. When we study the brief life of Josiah we are struck by his reverence. He revered David (2 Chronicles 34:2; 2 Kings 22:2), the temple (2 Kings 22:3–7), the Book of the Law (2 Kings 22:8–11), Huldah, the prophetess (2 Kings 22:14—23:3), one of the unnamed dead prophets (2 Kings 23:17–18), and certainly the Passover celebration (2 Kings 23:21–23). Isn't this appreciation of the past unusual for one so young?

What about his vision for the future? Unfortunately Judah's future was exceedingly bleak. Josiah seemed convinced that Judah's future survival was dependent upon its return to the God of its past.

Unfortunately Josiah could not keep Judah from Babylonian captivity, but he tried very hard. He was not satisfied that he would be spared (2 Kings 22:19–20), he wanted the people he was leading to be spared also.

138

He was a man who loved people, a man of compassion. Jeremiah wrote of him: "The Lord blessed Josiah because he treated people right and saw to it that even the poor and those with special needs were helped" (Jeremiah 22:15–16, LB).

D. Decisive and Thorough. Josiah was not afraid to make decisions—sometimes radical ones. At the age of 16 he decided to seek the God of David and to do what was right in the sight of the Lord (2 Chronicles 34:1–2). When he was 20 years old he decided to destroy the practice of idolatry, keep the laws found in the Book, celebrate the Passover, renovate the temple and reinstitute the worship of Jehovah.

He did these things swiftly and thoroughly (2 Kings 23:2–3, 4–20; 2 Chronicles 34:3–7).

E. Organized and Committed. Josiah planned his work and worked his plan. He brought about change, but he was no wide–eyed revolutionary. He was much more like Mohandus Gandhi and Martin Luther King, Jr. than Huey Newton and Stokely Carmichael. He did not destroy for the sake of destruction and vengeance. He destroyed so he could build. He gathered around him people who were skilled in specific, critically needed areas and trustworthy in character.

Is it possible to read the life and work of Josiah in 2 Kings 22 and 23 without being impressed that this brother was organized? Josiah seems to have acted only after he gave careful thought to the what, who, when, where and how of the project. Josiah was effective because he planned his work and worked his plan.

Perhaps the motivating power behind all of Josiah's effectiveness was his personal commitment and the commitment he inspired. First of all he was committed to God. He was committed to the will of God, the way of God, the Word of God, and the worship of God.

Finally, Josiah was committed to the people of God. It was said of Manasseh, Josiah's grandfather, that he "seduced Judah...to do more evil than the nations whom the Lord had

139

destroyed before the children of Israel" (2 Chronicles 33:2). But Josiah loved his people, shared his personal wealth with them and went down in Jewish history as the king who "was just and fair in all his dealings...He saw to it that justice and help were given to the poor and the needy..." (Jeremiah 22:15–16, LB).

Josiah loved his people and committed himself to their well–being. They in turn were committed to him and followed his leadership. And though the little nation was poised on the brink of disaster, because of his leadership Judah enjoyed a few years of peace and prosperity.

SCRIPTURE FOCUS

2 CHRONICLES 34:1 Josiah was eight years old when he began to reign, and he reigned in Jerusalem one and thirty years.

2 And he did that which was right in the sight of the Lord, and walked in the ways of David his father, and declined neither to the right hand, nor to the left.

3 For in the eighth year of his reign, while he was yet young, he began to seek after the God of David his father: and in the twelfth year he began to purge Judah and Jerusalem from the high places, and the groves, and the carved images, and the molten images.

8 Now in the eighteenth year of his reign, when he had purged the land, and the house, he sent Shaphan the son of Azaliah, and Maaseiah the governor of the city, and Joah the son of Joahaz the recorder, to repair the house of the Lord his God.

15 And Hilkiah answered and said to Shaphan the scribe, I have found the book of the law in the

*house of the Lord. And Hilkiah delivered the book
to Shaphan.*

*18 Then Shaphan the scribe told the king, saying,
Hilkiah the priest hath given me a book. And
Shaphan read it before the king.*

*19 And it came to pass, when the king had heard
the words of the law, that he rent his clothes.*

*20 And the king commanded Hilkiah, and
Ahikam the son of Shaphan, and Abdon the son of
Micah, and Shaphan the scribe, and Asaiah a
servant of the king's, saying,*

*21 Go, inquire of the Lord for me, and for them
that are left in Israel and in Judah, concerning
the words of the book that is found: for great is
the wrath of the Lord that is poured out upon us,
because our fathers have not kept the word of the
Lord, to do after all that is written in this book.*

*22 And Hilkiah, and they that the king had ap-
pointed, went to Huldah the prophetess, the wife
of Shallum the son of Tikvath, the son of Hasrah,
keeper of the wardrobe; (now she dwelt in
Jerusalem in the college:) and they spake to her
to that effect.*

*23 And she answered them, Thus saith the Lord
God of Israel, Tell ye the man that sent you to me.*

*27 Because thine heart was tender, and thou
didst humble thyself before God, when thou hear-
dest his words against this place, and against the
inhabitants thereof, and humbledst thyself before
me, and didst rend thy clothes, and weep before
me; I have even heard thee also, saith the Lord.*

*28 Behold, I will gather thee to thy fathers, and
thou shalt be gathered to thy grave in peace,
neither shall thine eyes see all the evil that I will*

141

bring upon this place, and upon the inhabitants of the same. So they brought the king word again.

2 CHRONICLES 35:1 Moreover Josiah kept a passover unto the Lord in Jerusalem: and they killed the passover on the fourteenth day of the first month.

17 And the children of Israel that were present kept the passover at that time, and the feast of unleavened bread seven days.

23 And the archers shot at king Josiah; and the king said to his servants, Have me away; for I am sore wounded.

24 His servants therefore took him out of that chariot, and put him in the second chariot that he had; and they brought him to Jerusalem, and he died, and was buried in one of the sepulchres of his fathers. And all Judah and Jerusalem mourned for Josiah.

25 And Jeremiah lamented for Josiah: and all the singing men and the singing women spake of Josiah in their lamentations to this day, and made them an ordinance in Israel: and, behold, they are written in the lamentations.

SCRIPTURE SEARCH

1. Josiah's work. He…

   a. rooted out _____.

   b. repaired the _____.

   c. restored the _____ to prominence.

   d. revived the celebration of the _____.

   e. restored _____.

2. Josiah's character. He was…

a. humble and _____.

b. _____ and generous.

c. reverent and _____.

d. decisive and _____.

e. _____ and committed.

The African American Connection

We can learn at least three lessons from our study of Josiah's life that will help us in our struggle for survival and success.

1. Handicapped

First, we see that it is possible to start life handicapped and still do well. Josiah was handicapped by a very bad family reputation.

2. Young, Black and Serious

A second lesson from Josiah's life is that it is possible to be young (2 Kings 22:1), Black (see the *Black Biblical Heritage*) and serious about God (see 2 Chronicles 34:3).[2] How exciting and challenging for those of us who work with African American youth.

3. Committed to Change

A final lesson from Josiah's life is that it is possible for one committed person to make a positive difference.

We know that Josiah did not change the religious and social behavior of Judah singlehandedly. We know that he had the assistance of such people as Hilkiah, Shaphan, and Huldah.

We also know that the Prophets Nahum, Habakkuk, Zephaniah and Jeremiah were carrying on their ministry during Josiah's administration.

But Josiah, young, Black and handicapped by his family background, committed himself to God. And through him, God made a positive difference throughout the kingdom.

4. What Do You Think?

A. What reputation did Josiah's father and grandfather have? How did Josiah respond to their gift? What reputation have your ancestors left for you? How have you responded to their gift?

B. Are there any young Josiahs and Josephines in your congregation? How can you encourage them to become "salt" and "light" in their environments?

C. In what five ways did the nation of Israel change under Josiah's leaderships? What can African American leaders learn from Josiah's leadership characteristics?

D. Draw two or three parallels between Josiah and African American leaders of the 20th century.

CHAPTER TWELVE

HOPE IN SPITE OF TEARS

LET'S DISCOVER . . .

Can God use a "cry baby" to help society realize its immorality and rottenness, its doom and demise? Let's discover how God uses water–heads and tear fountains to help us see our crying needs, our desperate condition; our source of hope.

JEREMIAH:
Hope in Spite of Tears

Dr. Kenneth Hammonds
Jeremiah 1:1-10; 9:1-2; Lamentations 3:21-26

The Prophet Jeremiah was a man who experienced great suffering and who understood the problems of seeking to do that which is right. He was a man who stood for his convictions no matter what the consequences. He had a great burden for his people and was not ashamed to express a deep, emotional concern for his people. He understood what it meant to stand alone against the injustices of the government. Jeremiah teaches us that God is faithful in the midst of any trial.

Jeremiah's Roots

Jeremiah was born into a priestly family in the little town of Anathoth, about three miles northeast of Jerusalem, Judah's capital city (Jeremiah 1:1). If Jeremiah was called to ministry between the ages of 16 and 18, then the date of his birth would be around 640 B.C. His father was Hilkiah (1:1), who is said by tradition to be a descendant of the priestly line of Abiathar, one of David's priests. Abiathar was a descendant of Eli, the last great priest before Saul, Israel's first king. Even though the priests and prophets of Israel were permitted to marry and have children, Jeremiah was commanded by God not to marry and was told that he would be childless (16:2). This command was given to emphasize Jeremiah's message that God's judgment would come through the Babylonians who would utterly destroy the city of Jerusalem and break up families.

146

The exact meaning of Jeremiah's Hebrew name *Yirmeyah* is uncertain, but at least two possibilities have been suggested: "The LORD (Yahweh) Exalts" or "The LORD (Yahweh) Throws." In a practical sense it means that it is Yahweh (God's name in Hebrew) who establishes and appoints. God appointed Jeremiah to deliver a message of repentance to the people of his time. Jeremiah suffered much from the hands of his own people, but he suffered realizing that he was "appointed" by God and therefore comforted by God.

Jeremiah's Times

Jeremiah lived in very turbulent times. The surrounding governments were politically unstable and the people of Israel were religiously unstable. During the reigns of the last seven kings of Judah, the people vacillated between the worship of the true God of Israel and the worship of Baal and other gods (1:16; 7:9). They lived immoral lives and inflicted many injustices upon the poor.

A capsule view of the history of Israel may assist us in understanding the times of Jeremiah. Around 900 B.C. the nation of Israel was divided into two separate nations. The Northern Kingdom (10 tribes) under Jeroboam I was called Israel, and the Southern Kingdom (two tribes, Judah and Benjamin) under Rehoboam, Solomon's son, was called Judah.

The Northern Kingdom left the worship of the Lord and in 722 B.C., the Assyrians invaded the country and destroyed Samaria, its capital city. The Southern Kingdom was spared by God because they were faithful to Him. However, during the time of Jeremiah's ministry from 626 B.C. to about 580 B.C. Judah was also unfaithful to God. Jeremiah and his contemporary prophets were sent to the nation of Judah to preach a message of repentance and restoration for their obedience, or a warning about suffering the judgment of God for their disobedience.

Two foreign nations, Egypt and Babylonia, stand out during the time of Jeremiah. They competed for the land of Israel. They were enemies with one another. Assyria, the power that had destroyed the Northern Kingdom, was weakening at the time of Jeremiah's call in 626 B.C. which was during the reign of Josiah. The last five kings of the Southern Kingdom were:

Josiah 640–609 B.C.

Jehoahaz 609

Jehoiakim 609–598

Jehoiachin 598–597

Zedekiah 597–586

Of these kings only Josiah was a just king and did that which was pleasing in the sight of the Lord.

Jeremiah's Writings

The Prophet Jeremiah is the author of the Book of Jeremiah, one of the longest in the Bible. Because of his autobiographical book, we know more about Jeremiah's life than any other prophet in the Bible. The 52 chapters of the Book of Jeremiah are not in chronological order. Jeremiah uses many literary divices. Much of the book is poetry and the beauty of his poetry can be seen in any good English translation that recognizes the original Hebrew text as poetic.

The Prophet Jeremiah is also the author of the very emotional and personal Book of Lamentations. The book records the prophet's grief as he witnesses the suffering and pain inflicted upon his people by the Babylonian invasion of Jerusalem. Lamentations is composed entirely of various poems about the city's destruction and his acknowledgment of God's faithfulness in the midst of destruction.

Jeremiah's Ministry

Jeremiah was called to ministry in the thirteenth year of King Josiah's reign, around 626 B.C. His ministry continues slightly beyond the fall of Jerusalem in 586 B.C. At that time he was about 64 years old. How and when Jeremiah died are not certain, but Jewish tradition asserts that he was stoned to death in Egypt.

God's commission of Jeremiah recorded in Jeremiah chapter one is one of the most touching and dramatic in all of Scripture, recalling the experiences of Isaiah (Isaiah 6) and the Apostle Paul (Acts 9). The Word of Yahweh to Jeremiah is recorded in the first chapter, verse 5. Jeremiah was appointed a prophet not just to Judah and nearby Jerusalem, but also to the surrounding nations.

His tasks were: "To root out and to pull down,

To destroy and to throw down,

To build and to plant" (v. 10).

Today we can apply this threefold ministry of Jeremiah to the ministry of the Church at the end of the 20th century as:

1. The evangelist—to root out and pull down the works of sin and Satan;

2. The prophet—to destroy and to throw down evil systems (whether economic, political, social, educational, or ecclesiastical);

3. The teacher—to build or develop people and to plant spiritual seeds.

Jeremiah's Message

Jeremiah's message seems to encompass more of the rooting out and throwing down than the building. His message was a call for the people to return to Yahweh, the God of the covenant, and to avoid the impending destruction of Jerusalem by Nebuchadnezzar who was leading the Babylonian army. If they did not repent then the city and the country would fall under God's judgment and suffer defeat. In chapter three, Jeremiah repeats the Word of God to Judah: "return to me." The Lord so beautifully entreats His people: "'Return, O backsliding children,' says the LORD; for I am married to you" (3:14).

Jeremiah had words of judgment against the surrounding nations of Egypt, the Philistines, Moabites, Ammonites, and

Edomites (chapters 46—49). Also included in the judgment of God were the cities of Damascus, Hamath, Arpad, Kedar, Hazor, Elam and Babylon, both the city and the nation (chapters 50—51). It seems as if God's message of judgment for the entire world was given to this single prophet.

However, it was not all bad news. Jeremiah looked into the future and revealed the nature of a "new covenant" which will be written in the minds and hearts of the people of God. The Church of Jesus Christ now enjoys the blessings of this new covenant made available to us by the life, death and resurrection of Jesus Christ (Luke 22:20; 1 Corinthians 10:16; 11:25–26; Hebrews 8:6—9:28).

Just like fire! Even though his message was unpleasant, Jeremiah could not stop preaching the Word of the Lord. In Jeremiah 20:9 the prophet waxes eloquent regarding the fiery message burning in the deepest recesses of his very being. This easily has become the most quoted passage of the Book of Jeremiah:

> "Then I said, 'I will not make mention of Him,
> Nor speak anymore in His name.' But His word
> was in my heart like a burning fire shut up in my
> bones; I was weary of holding it back, And I
> could not" (20:9).

God's spokesman: calling or curse? This harsh burning message was not well received. Persecution became so difficult for Jeremiah that in chapter 20 he poetically curses the very day of his birth and thereby questions his calling and his God. In this extended passage Jeremiah puts together a masterpiece of poetry just to curse his very existence on earth! It is important that you read the whole chapter.

Actually, Jeremiah could not curse the day he was born because God had already blessed it and sanctified him for service. Even as Balaam could not curse the blessed people of Israel (Numbers 23), Jeremiah's request too was void as Balaam himself noted in Numbers 23:20: "He has blessed, and I cannot reverse it." The call of God is great upon the instrument of God's Word. In Lamentations 3:22–23 Jeremiah observed:

> "Through the LORD's mercies we are not con-
> sumed, Because His compassions fail not. They are
> new every morning; Great is Your faithfulness."

Jeremiah's Enemies and Problems

Jeremiah had a few friends. His most faithful companion, his secretary Baruch, was responsible for the compilation of the Book of Jeremiah. However, it seems as if Jeremiah spent more time with his enemies than with his friends. The enemies of Jeremiah were always after him and continually causing him problems. A listing of his enemies and problems can give us a new appreciation for this man's courage and remind us that the problems of leadership always carry a price.

1. He was called a traitor to his country and his people.
2. He was beaten.
3. He was placed in stocks.
4. He was imprisoned.
5. He was placed in a muddy dungeon to die. He was subsequently saved from death by a Black man, an Ethiopian (Cushite) officer (or eunuch) named Ebed–Melech (Jeremiah 38:7–13).
6. The false prophets were his enemies.
7. He was hated for 25 years by all the kings and most of the leaders after Josiah. Jehoiakim even cut up his prophetic scrolls and burned them in the fire.
8. Even his brothers and relatives were against him.
9. He was taken to Egypt against his will.

Jeremiah's many difficulties remind us of the power of God to keep us strong in the midst of great difficulty. His endurance and fortitude are examples to all Christians, especially those in leadership positions.

The Prophet Jeremiah possessed a conviction with inner strength and sensitivity that is unparalleled in all the prophets of Scripture. He possessed an unwavering courage and dedication to the living God. And even though his message was hard, he had a soft heart for the people of God and tears were often a part of his message (Jeremiah 9:1). It is for this reason that he is known as the "weeping prophet." He did not want to see his people suffer but wanted them to enjoy the blessings of the Lord.

SCRIPTURE FOCUS

JEREMIAH 1:1 The words of Jeremiah the son of Hilkiah, of the priests that were in Anathoth in the land of Benjamin:

2 To whom the word of the Lord came in the days of Josiah the son of Amon king of Judah, in the thirteenth year of his reign.

3 It came also in the days of Jehoiakim the son of Josiah king of Judah, unto the end of the eleventh year of Zedekiah the son of Josiah king of Judah, unto the carrying away of Jerusalem captive in the fifth month.

4 Then the word of the Lord came unto me, saying,

5 Before I formed thee in the belly I knew thee; and before thou camest forth out of the womb I sanctified thee, and I ordained thee a prophet unto the nations.

6 Then said I, Ah, Lord God! behold, I cannot speak: for I am a child.

7 But the Lord said unto me, Say not, I am a child: for thou shalt go to all that I shall send thee, and whatsoever I command thee thou shalt speak.

8 Be not afraid of their faces: for I am with thee to deliver thee, saith the Lord.

9 Then the Lord put forth his hand, and touched my mouth. And the Lord said unto me, Behold, I have put my words in thy mouth.

10 See, I have this day set thee over the nations and over the kingdoms, to root out, and to pull down, and to destroy, and to throw down, to build, and to plant.

JEREMIAH 9:1 Oh that my head were waters, and mine eyes a fountain of tears, that I might weep day and night for the slain of the daughter of my people!

2 Oh that I had in the wilderness a lodging place of wayfaring men; that I might leave my people, and go from them! for they be all adulterers, an assembly of treacherous men.

LAMENTATIONS 3:21 This I recall to my mind, therefore have I hope.

22 It is of the Lord's mercies that we are not consumed, because his compassions fail not.

23 They are new every morning: great is thy faithfulness.

24 The Lord is my portion, saith my soul; therefore will I hope in him.

25 The Lord is good unto them that wait for him, to the soul that seeketh him.

26 It is good that a man should both hope and quietly wait for the salvation of the Lord.

SCRIPTURE SEARCH

Let's play "Bible Jeopardy."

CLUE	QUESTION
1. A prophet of hope.	A. Who was _____?
2. Jeremiah's hometown.	B. What was _____?
3. Jeremiah's other book.	C. What is _____?
4. "To build and plant."	D. What was Jeremiah's _____?
5. "Return to Yahweh!"	E. What was Jeremiah's _____?

The African American Connection

Here are some thoughts about how some of the verses in the Book of Jeremiah and some of the experiences in his life can make Jeremiah come alive with relevancy for the contemporary problems and concerns of today's Christians.

1. Abortion

How does Jeremiah 1:5 help to discuss the hotly debated issue of abortion? When does life begin? How would your beliefs about God as the ultimate Creator of human life and the Lover of human beings affect your personal views on abortion?

2. Leadership

Many people believe that a man or woman needs to be an older person to be accepted as a valid leader. Others believe that God does not call teenagers to active ministry to adults. What does God's response to Jeremiah in Jeremiah 1:7 reveal about a young person's potential? Are the youth of today really the Church of tomorrow or are they the Church of today?

Do you think that those under age 21 are the only ones "qualified" to minister to their own generation? Were there any famous Bible leaders who were over 40, but who were able to relate well to young people?

3. Spiritual Development

The people of Israel needed to be shaped and molded by God. Even though the people were marred by their sins (v. 4), God wanted to make them into usable vessels of effective service.

Our young people are being molded by the thought processes of the mass media and peer groups. What if we were determined to consciously and deliberately mold our young people by God's Word and principles of successful living? What strategies could the church use to make Bible study more exciting than television?

In what sense is the molding of our younger generation important to the survival of our people? What are you personally doing to assist in the formation of the next generation?

FOOTNOTES

Chapter Two - Hosea
1. James Luther Mays, *Hosea* (Philadelphia: Westminster, 1969), p. 6.

2. George I. Robinson, *The 12 Minor Prophets* (Grand Rapids: Baker Book House, 1990), p. 26.

3. Mays, *op. cit.,* p. 11.

Chapter Three - Amos
1. Burlan A. Sizemore, Jr., *The Centuries of Decline, 5 vols.* (Nashville: Convention Press, 1970), p. 40.

2. Kyle M. Yates, *Preaching from the Prophets* (Nashville: Broadman Press, 1942), p. 52.

3. *Ibid.,* p. 51.

4. Irving L. Jensen, *Jensen's Survey of the Old Testament* (Chicago: Moody Press, 1975), p. 397.

Chapter Four - Abraham
1. Louis I. Newman, editor, *The Talmudic Anthology* (New York: Behrman House, 1945), p. 522.

Chapter Five - Moses
1. Aryeh Kaplan, *The Living Torah* (New York: Moznaim, 1981), p. 145.

Chapter Six - Deborah
1. George Arthur Buttrick, "Deborah," *The Interpreter's Dictionary of the Bible, Volume 1* (1962), p. 809.

2. Herbert Lockyer, *All The Women in the Bible* (Grand Rapids: Zondervan, 1967), p. 40.

3. *Ibid.*

4. Buttrick, p. 809.

5. Lockyer, p. 41.

6. *Ibid.*

7. Bennie E. Goodwin, *The Effective Leader* (Atlanta: Goodpatrick, 1989), p. 11.

8. Roger Hatch and Frank Watkins, *Reverend Jesse L. Jackson: Straight From the Heart* (Philadelphia: Fortress Press, 1987), p. xx.

9. *Ibid.*

Chapter Seven - Samuel

1. There were three "pilgrimage festivals" to which every Israelite man was required to attend: a) Passover and the Feast of Unleavened Bread, b) the Feast of Week or the "Day of Pentecost," which was held 50 days after the Sabbath of the Passover, and c) the Feast of Tabernacles, which was held in the seventh month, to commemorate the wanderings from Egypt to Canaan.

2. Many biblical names of individuals, nations and places have Blackness explicit in their meanings. "Phinehas" means "the Negro" or "the Nubian." This was common practice in northeast Africa (where Israel is) and various other parts of Africa. Even during the years of European colonialism, children were not named until they were born. See Chiekh Diop, *The African Origin of Civilization* (Chicago: Hill, 1974), pp. 146-148. See also Walter Arthur McCray, *Black Presence in the Bible, vol. 1* (Chicago: Black Light Fellowship), p. 20.

3. Philistines were also a Hamitic (Black African descended) people like the Nubians and Egyptians (Genesis 10:6-14). They were evidently mariners who voyaged from lands north of the Aegean Sea via Crete to Palestine. See McCray, p. 76.

4. In verse 6 of the *Septuagint* (Lxx) and *Vulgate* (vg) translations, reference is made to rats or mice in connection with destruction in Ashdod while the Ark was there. This is supported by the trespass offering made by the Philistines in 6:1-11.

5. Circuit-riding preachers are familiar to the African American church. Many freed slaves earned their living riding from town to town preaching in small churches, tents or wagon trains. Some of the most famous African American ministers rode circuits at some point in their lives. Bishop Richard Allen, founder of the A.M.E. Church, is an example.

Chapter Eight - David

1. George A. Bedrock, "David," *The Interpreters Dictionary of the Bible, Volume 1* (1962), p. 753.

2. *Ibid.*, p. 775.

3. Finus J. Dake, *Dake's Annotated Reference Bible* (Lawrenceville: Dake Bible Sale), p. 332.

4. Herbert Lockyer, *All the Men of the Bible* (Grand Rapids: Zondervan,

1958), pp. 89-90.

5. *Ibid.*, pp. 90-91.

6. Bennie Goodwin, *The Effective Leader* (Atlanta: Goodpatrick, 1989), pp. 7-10.

Chapter Ten - Elijah

1. W. Milligan, *Elijah, His Life and Times* **(Old Tappan, New Jersey: Revell, n.d.), p. 2.**

2. C. F. Keil and F. Delitzsch, *Commentary on the Old Testament in Ten Volumes* (Grand Rapids: Eerdman, 1980), p. 286.

3. *Ibid.*, p. 246.

4. *Ibid.*, p. 258.

5. *Ibid.*, p. 19.

Chapter Eleven - Josiah

1. Bennie Goodwin, *The Effective Leader* **(Atlanta: Goodpatrick, 1989), p. 11.**

2. John L. Johnson, *The Black Biblical Heritage* (Nashville: Winston-Derek, 1991 edition), pp. 145, 175. According to Johnson, Josiah was a descendant of Queen Jezebel who was "a beautiful black women from Tyre of the Zidonians (Phoenicians)," and the Zidonians were descendants from Canaan's first son, Zidon.

BIBLIOGRAPHY

Anderson, Bernard W. *Understanding the Old Testament.* Englewood Cliffs, New Jersey: Prentice–Hall, 1975.

Benson, Clarence H. *Old Testament Survey.* Wheaton: Evangelical Teacher Training Association, 1976.

Benware, Paul N. *Survey of the Old Testament.* Chicago: Moody Press, 1988.

Blacklock, E. M. *Today's Handbook of Bible Characters.* Minneapolis: Bethany House, 1979.

Blenkinsopp, Joseph. *A History of Prophesy in Israel.* Philadelphia: Westminster, 1983.

Craigie, Peter C. *Twelve Prophets, Vol. 1 The Daily Study Bible Series.* Philadelphia: Westminster Press, 1984.

Davis, John J., and Whitcomb, John C. *A History of Israel–From Conquest to Exile.* Grand Rapids: Baker Book House, 1974.

Diggs, Ellen Irene. *Black Chronology.* Boston: Hall, 1988.

Diop, Chiekh Anta. *The African Origin of Civilization.* Chicago: Hill, 1974.

Dunston, Alfred, Jr. *The Black Man in the Old Testament and its World.* Philadelphia: Dorrance, 1974.

Hailey, Homer. *A Commentary on The Minor Prophets.* Grand Rapids: Baker Book House, 1987.

Halley, Henry H. *Halley's Bible Handbook.* Grand Rapids: Zondervan, 1965.

Herrmann, Siegfried. *A History of Israel in Old Testament Times.* Philadelphia: Fortress Press, 1981.

Jensen, Irving L. *Jensen's Survey of the Old Testament.* Chicago: Moody Press, 1978.

Josephas, Flavius. *The Complete Works of Flavius Josephas.* Translated by William Whiston. Grand Rapids: Kreagel, 1991.

Linburg, James. *The Prophets and the Powerless.* Atlanta: Knox, 1978.

Lockyer, Herbert. *All the Kings and Queens of the Bible.* Grand Rapids: Zondervan, 1961.

Lockyer, Herbert. *All the Women of the Bible.* Grand Rapids: Zondervan, 1967.

McKinley, Harry. *Reading the Old Testament Prophets Today.* Atlanta: Knox, 1979.

Noveck, Simon, Editor. *Great Jewish Personalities.* Washington: B'nai

B'rith, 1959.

Peterson, David. *Prophecy in Israel.* Philadelphia: Fortress, 1987.

Pusay, E. B. *The Minor Prophets: A Commentary.* Grand Rapids: Baker Book House, 1982.

Rawlinson, George. *Men of the Bible: The Kings of Israel and Judah.* New York: Revell, n.d.

Robinson, George I. *The Minor Prophets.* Grand Rapids: Baker Book House, 1990.

Shannon, David. *The Old Testament Experience of Faith.* Valley Forge: Judson, 1977.

Sizemore, B. A., Jr. *The Centuries of Decline.* Nashville: Convention Press, 1970.

Steinsaltz, Adin. *Biblical Images.* New York: Basic Books, 1984.

Walvoord, John F. *The Bible Knowledge Commentary: Old Testament.* Wheaton: Victor Books, 1985.

Wiesel, Elie. *Messengers of God.* New York: Summit Books, 1976.

Wilmore, Gayraud S. *Black Religion and Black Radicalism.* Maryknoll, New York: Orbis Books, 1990.